Praise for 7...

The ABCS of Coping with Anxiety is written in a beautifully straightforward, uncomplicated way that allows the reader to follow both its instruction and the author's thought process with ease.

I am not a cognitive behavioural therapist and, as such, I would look for root causes to illuminate the belief system that created the anxiety in the first place. James Cowart helps the reader to recognise their triggers and, by doing so, assists them to interrupt their self-defeating anxiety patterns. Anxiety is often caused – as is eloquently explained in the book – by lack of control, however I believe the direct, descriptive ABCS approach will help many in taking back some of that control by better recognising what they can and can't influence.

The ideas and explanations are clear and I have no doubt *The ABCS of Coping with Anxiety* will be a trusted companion for many in seeking coping strategies for their anxiety.

Alison Knowles, author of *Ollie and His Super Powers*

The ABCS of Coping with Anxiety is a concise, clear, specific and practical user-friendly guide for sufferers of various anxiety issues. The author has combined findings from the best evidence-based outcome research on anxiety treatment with the real-world knowledge that can only be gained from years of actual clinical experience treating anxiety patients. The result is a compact guide to lead the reader through a sequence of four practical steps – the ABCS.

Intended as a self-help guide for those who cannot readily access professional help (for any number of reasons), the ABCS approach focuses on the key treatment steps that clinical research evidence has confirmed are necessary, if not essential, for recovery from debilitating anxiety problems. The guide would also prove useful to those searching for the most effective kind of professional help

with their anxiety by ensuring that key evidence-based treatment components are effectively covered in sessions with their therapist.

Although symptoms may differ across the anxiety disorders spectrum, the book lays out the core treatment components that have been found to be widely effective. The ABCS approach, however, does also discuss, explain, and provide more specific suggestions for dealing with various symptoms as they differ among the anxiety disorders. This helps readers to personalize their coping program to meet their unique needs and circumstances.

Having a book like *The ABCS of Coping with Anxiety* available addresses several practical real-life needs facing sufferers of debilitating anxiety. Some sufferers live too far away from professional providers; others cannot afford professional help; others may feel too shy or embarrassed to seek help; and others may wish to try to master their anxiety on their own. All can benefit from reading *The ABCS of Coping with Anxiety.*

Galen Alessi, PhD, Professor Emeritus, Clinical Psychology Doctoral Program and Clinic, Western Michigan University

The ABCS of Coping with Anxiety is the most concise but comprehensive book that I have read on the subject, and will be useful to both those living with anxiety and the therapists who treat them.

It is a book that can be used by the individual alone or with their therapist – and might also be very useful for those attending self-help groups. I highly recommend *The ABCS of Coping with Anxiety* because of its logical organization, allowing the reader to clearly understand what is necessary to help them recover from anxiety.

Leo A. Kominek, PhD, retired scientist and psychologist

James has simplified the complex treatment for anxiety and made it accessible to all, providing a good foundation for understanding what anxiety really is and what works in overcoming it.

If anxiety is holding you back from living the life you want to live, *The ABCS of Coping with Anxiety* offers evidence-based techniques for facing your fears – whether you're doing it alone, or alongside a therapist.

Dr. Hazel Harrison, clinical psychologist

I've read many books on CBT over the years but this is without doubt my favourite!

Although it is primarily intended for sufferers of stress and anxiety disorders, I believe professionals will also find it a helpful resource, full of clear, easy-to-understand explanations to use with patients. I love James Cowart's crystal clear style, which never sounds in any way condescending. He offers the reader hope and reassurance that the practical coping skills will prove effective when they stay with the approach.

Lynda Hudson, clinical hypnotherapist and author of
More Scripts and Strategies in Hypnotherapy

I can't give *The ABCS of Coping with Anxiety* enough praise. James Cowart has written a most engaging volume: one that is succinct, comprehensive and straightforward to read.

Appealing to both the client and therapist alike, it provides sensible approaches to working with anxiety disorders that come from a CBT perspective, without being afraid to dip its metaphorical toes into the third wave therapies and beyond. This engaging, pluralistic framework is refreshing as we are brought back to the often-forgotten foundations of anxiety management and are encouraged to build effective strategies around the author's ABCS model. James provides many interesting and useful case examples that guide the reader through the client exercises, highlighting their immediate relevance to effectively managing a variety of anxiety disorders.

This honest and realistic book has something for everyone, including the client's partner and family members.

Peter Mabbutt, Vice Principal, London College of Clinical Hypnosis, Vice President, British Society of Clinical Hypnosis

The ABCS of Coping with Anxiety is a remarkable read. It is as if the reader is actually speaking with James Cowart, whose voice is authentic, highly respectful and, most importantly, supportive as he provides carefully scaffolded guidance to those in need of coping skills to manage anxiety and stress on a day-to-day basis.

The book appears to be beguilingly simple, although it is clearly a rich source of evidence-based strategies and tactics with which to approach the management of anxiety. James provides academic references and resources for those suffering the effects of anxiety, and for mental health professionals who wish to delve more deeply into specific aspects of dealing with anxiety.

At the heart of *The ABCS of Coping with Anxiety* is a focus on the applications of the coping skills to specific anxiety-related problems – all garnered from over 40 years' practice as a psychologist using cognitive behavioral therapy. It also includes coping skills for dealing with anxiety associated with depression and anger outbursts and provides specific tools and exercises to facilitate the implementation of these skills.

An invaluable guide for those working alone or with a mental health professional, *The ABCS of Coping with Anxiety* takes the reader on a journey and provides a straightforward roadmap with real-life examples, exercises and tools designed to strengthen and reinforce the reader's ability to deal with fear and reduce anxiety.

Sandra Greenberg, PhD, Vice President – Research and Advisory Services, Professional Examination Service

One of the most difficult aspects of suffering with stress and anxiety is knowing where to start the process of learning to cope. In *The ABCS of Coping with Anxiety*, James Cowart provides an excellent point of reference to help you understand what will bring calm and composure back into your life.

You will learn the fundamental reasons why anxiety is affecting you, and how your current coping skills can be improved, once you start to employ the ABCS method. Starting with an acceptance of the things you cannot control, you will learn how to become more resilient and stop the cycle of anxiety from perpetuating.

In this incredibly helpful resource, James presents an abundance of techniques and methods to help guide you and provides log sheets to enable you to chart your journey along the way. Most especially, for those who are suffering with severe anxiety, such as OCD, general anxiety disorder, social anxiety, phobias or PTSD, this book offers some really useful practical help and explanations. There are also case study examples of how the methods work, as well as the very helpful addition of information relating to the effects of anxiety, such as depression and anger.

Having worked for 25 years with clients dealing with some of the difficulties explored in this book, I wish this resource had been available earlier as it would have been a well-used reference. I commend the author for his dedication in sharing his knowledge and I highly recommend *The ABCS of Coping with Anxiety* to students and fellow professionals alike.

Dr. Tom Barber, founder, Contemporary College of Therapeutic Studies, educator, psychotherapist, coach and bestselling author

James Cowart, PhD

The ABCs of COPING with ANXIETY

Using CBT to manage stress and anxiety

Crown House Publishing Limited
www.crownhouse.co.uk

First published by

Crown House Publishing Ltd
Crown Buildings, Bancyfelin, Carmarthen, Wales, SA33 5ND, UK
www.crownhouse.co.uk

and

Crown House Publishing Company LLC
PO Box 2223, Williston, VT 05495
www.crownhousepublishing.com

Crown House Publishing has no responsibility for the persistence or accuracy of URLs
for external or third-party websites referred to in this publication, and does not
guarantee that any content on such websites is, or will remain, accurate or appropriate.

British Library Cataloguing-in-Publication Data
A catalogue entry for this book is available from the British Library.

Print ISBN 978-178583167-6
Mobi ISBN 978-178583260-4
ePub ISBN 978-178583261-1
ePDF ISBN 978-178583262-8

LCCN 2017944326

Printed and bound in the UK by
Gomer Press, Llandysul, Ceredigion

This book is dedicated to the many patients that I have seen over the years. I have learned as much from them as they have learned from me. The ideas in this book were made much better by their reactions and their feedback. Their courage in facing their fears is something to admire. I owe them a debt of gratitude. Also, please be assured that throughout the book I have changed all names and key identifying information to protect their confidentiality.

Acknowledgments

I want to acknowledge the positive influence of all those listed in the bibliography. Throughout my professional career I have often depended on the published work of others such as Joseph Wolpe, Albert Ellis, Aaron Beck, David Burns, David H. Barlow, Edna Foa and also Martin Seligman. In addition, I want to point out the positive influence of my professors at the University of Michigan, such as Edwin Thomas, Dick Stuart, Bob Carter and Joseph Himle and, of course, the chairperson of my doctoral committee at Western Michigan University: Jack Michael, as well as the other members of my committee: Dick Malott, Brian Iwata and Howard Farris. In particular, I want to thank Leo Kominek for his thoughtful insights over the years and for many helpful comments on earlier drafts of this work. I also want to thank Galen Alessi and Bonnie Bowden for their early input. Finally, I especially want to thank my wife, Lynne Cowart, who is always the final reviewer of my written work and the best supporter of my positive endeavors.

CONTENTS

Introduction

Perhaps you have picked up this book because you have not yet found adequate help in dealing with the excessive feelings of stress and anxiety you may be experiencing. My aim in this book is to share with you coping skills that will enable you to manage your excessive stress and anxiety on a day-to-day basis. In my clinical experience, the consequences of untreated problems with anxiety can be devastating. Untreated anxiety problems tend to spread and grow through fear conditioning and eventually can take over a person's life. As this worsens, it is not uncommon for individuals to begin to experience outbursts of anger and growing depression as well. In an attempt to escape and avoid the stress and misery they are experiencing, an individual may begin to smoke, abuse alcohol, take illegal or prescription drugs or engage in other distracting, but ultimately self-defeating, behavior. These excessive activities may make them feel better, even if only for a few minutes, but will have detrimental long-term consequences. These individuals may eventually suffer from a wide variety of limitations and problems that negatively affect all aspects of their lives. Alternatively, I have seen a great number of people successfully treat their anxiety problems by learning key coping skills from cognitive behavioral therapy (CBT). This form of therapy is based on helping people change their behavior and their thoughts and beliefs. It is this particular form of evidence-based therapy that underpins the ABCS outlined in this book.

So what do we mean by the term anxiety? There are a number of terms we commonly use to describe the nature of an anxiety disorder: e.g., stress, worry, panic and fear. I think of panic as being similar to the height of fear. Anxiety is often less intense than that, but still involves unpleasant feelings of stress and tension throughout the body that can last for a prolonged period of time. Worry refers to the thoughts that pass through our brains that can increase the unpleasant feelings associated with anxiety. You may also have heard people talk about the fight or flight (or fight, flight or freeze) response. This refers to the set of changes that happen within the brain and the body when an animal (or a human) is in real danger. When danger strikes, the brain reacts with automatic stimulation of the amygdala and hypothalamus, which results in adrenaline and other stress hormones being secreted into the bloodstream. The heart rate goes up and bodily functions not needed in an emergency are slowed or stopped (e.g., digestion). All these types of biological changes are designed to help the body deal with a perceived danger by preparing it for confrontation or running away (or freezing and hiding). The freeze element is our biological response when the situation is deemed so dangerous that the first two options will be ineffective. These responses happen automatically and require no conscious thinking. The fight or flight response evolved for good reason: to keep us safe from danger. It may be surprising to learn that anxiety is not necessarily always a problem. The ability to get anxious is a normal part of our human nature. Without this response our distant ancestors who lived in a physically dangerous world would probably not have survived long enough to reproduce. At a young age, they would have impulsively blundered into dangerous situations and perished, and we would not have had the chance to live. Our biological programming evolved to keep us safe.

All animals have this fight or flight response. However, humans can also use language to trigger it. Imagine a small group of early humans approaching a watering hole. A keen-sighted member of the group sees a lion approaching and immediately feels a rush of emotion as his fight or flight response is triggered. Almost as fast, he whispers "lion" to the others. They all feel a similar rush of emotion, before they see the lion, and they all automatically prepare to fight or run away, since hiding won't work in this situation.

The word, and the thought of the lion, is enough to trigger this process, without them needing to see the object of their fear. The individuals in alert groups like this survived long enough to pass their genes on to later humans. The key point is that in humans, language and thoughts can also trigger emotions.

The fight or flight response has evolved to keep us safe, but if it gets triggered in situations where there is no real danger then problems occur. One good way to think of an anxiety disorder is as a pattern of false alarms that persistently trigger our fight or flight response (partially or completely). The false alarms may be in the external environment or within us – in our own thoughts and language. The alarms are false because the individual is in no real, physical danger, but the sense of danger and the feelings of fear and anxiety are completely real.[1] To use the lion example, it wouldn't matter whether we were stood in front of the animal, or whether we had merely heard the word "lion," the stress response would be as palpable as if we were about to be attacked by it.

Priming us to run away from a lion is clearly a useful function of these anxiety inducing hormones. The problem with anxiety is that human beings can also become anxious in a way that doesn't serve a useful purpose. Humans have more complex brains than other animals. Our brains mean we are able to think about and imagine lots of possibilities. Presumably, dogs and cats don't worry a lot about what might happen in the future. Humans can use their more complex brains to think about and plan for the future, which of course can be a very good thing. However, our more complex brains also give us the opportunity to worry and get anxious about things that we have no control over, leading to the serious problems known as anxiety disorders. Learning to accept what we can and cannot control is one of the first steps in over-coming problems with anxiety.

Research presented by the National Institute of Mental Health (NIMH) shows that 18% of adults in the United States experi-ence anxiety disorders each year, and 23% of those cases are considered "severe." According to some research, of all the adults

---

1   For more on this see Barlow (2002).

in the United States who suffer from an anxiety disorder each year, only 13% receive even minimally adequate treatment.[2] Globally, problems with anxiety are very common and can be severe. It seems clear that a lot of people who suffer with anxiety problems do not get appropriate treatment. That may not be especially comforting to you as you begin to move forward in coping with your own anxiety, but hopefully in the future the availability of effective treatment will catch up with people's needs. In 2008, the National Health Service in England began a large initiative to expand the availability of CBT, but unfortunately this is not currently typical of most other countries around the world.[3]

The primary causes of serious problems with anxiety include: inherited genetic predisposition, negative childhood and adolescent experiences, past emotional traumas and current life stressors. An anxiety disorder is not a sign of "weakness of character" and has nothing to do with an individual's morality or courage. In fact, these negative cultural myths sometimes prevent individuals from getting the treatment they need. I have worked with many patients who have had to overcome these types of prejudices from bosses, friends and even close family members before they could even begin treatment. This social stigma is another reason why only a small percentage of people with anxiety problems get appropriate treatment.

If for whatever reason you can't get adequate access to an appropriate therapist, the skills you can learn from this book will form a good basis for you to begin to manage your anxiety. This book attempts to show how a set of easy to remember coping skills can be applied to different anxiety problems. The book is intended to be a teaching tool for individuals suffering from these problems and therefore minimizes excessive technical detail in favor of simplicity. The references within the book are there should you wish to read more about a specific aspect of anxiety, although this

---

2 See for example Kessler et al. (2005). The latest updates to this prevalence data can be found at the web site maintained by the NIMH (www.nimh.nih.gov). A broader world view suggests that the current, prevalence of anxiety disorders in Euro/Anglo cultures around the world is at least 10% (Baxter et al., 2013).

3 See Clark (2011) for more information.

volume should equip you with all the basic information you need. If you are reading this as a mental health professional, there is a brief section in the back of the book which outlines how you might find the book useful in your practice. Overall, the book emphasizes the importance of using coping skills to directly face core fears (whether they are fears of imagined catastrophes, humiliating social situations or traumatic memories) and adjust to negative life changes, rather than allowing the anxiety to progress and result in more and more limitations and other related disorders.

Anxiety coping skills can be used with classic anxiety disorders, with common fears and phobias and also in other stressful situations (e.g., the break-up of a relationship, the diagnosis of a frightening medical condition, etc.). This book also teaches other sets of coping skills to help with the related emotional problems that so frequently accompany anxiety disorders: depression and impulsive and angry outbursts. All of the coping skills come from my reading of the professional literature combined with decades of clinical experience as a cognitive behavioral therapist and clinical supervisor, plus countless interactions with my colleagues. This book is addressed to you, as you work on your problems with anxiety, but it is also useful as a resource for the cognitive behavioral therapist. If you are working with a therapist, ask them if they would be willing to help you work through the book.

As the title suggests, I use the acronym ABCS (acceptance, breathing and relaxing, countering and staying with it) to help you remember the key skills. It is easy to forget things when you are feeling a lot of stress and that's when you really need to use these skills. I have found that each of the four coping skills is helpful for full recovery from problems with anxiety. While it is not possible to control what others think or do, and it is not possible to directly control our emotions, it is possible to learn and apply these coping skills. The ABCS are to be used to face feared situations, not to escape or avoid them. Of course you can use the same coping skills when unexpected situations trigger anxiety.

Regardless of the initial causes of your anxiety, some of it is now maintained by your own cognitions (e.g., your thoughts, beliefs and assumptions). In childhood, we learn so many behaviors, and this can include unrealistic and unhealthy thoughts. They are strengthened throughout later childhood and adolescence. Despite parents' and teachers' best efforts, children may learn and then internalize thoughts such as: "It's terrible if I make a mistake in front of others." "It is horrible if someone doesn't like what I do or say." "I can't cope like other people do." "It is a catastrophe if I feel anxious." Once these types of cognitions are internalized they can easily arise again throughout life, during moments of challenge. These cognitions then help to make you more anxious and distressed just at the time when you need your energies to focus on how to deal with the challenge. The A for acceptance and C for countering are to assist you in learning to think about yourself in a more healthy and realistic manner so that you can begin to challenge this cause of your anxiety.

On the other hand, some of your anxiety is now maintained by negative, fear-conditioned experiences from your past.[4] If you have experienced high levels of stress (also known as the fight, flight or freeze response) in given situations in the past then you may have been conditioned to feel some of that anxiety and fear in similar new situations. You can remedy this part of the problem by breaking the pattern and having many more experiences that you cope with more successfully. Each time you cope well it is like putting money in the bank with a compounding interest rate. Eventually the new experiences can overcome the effects of that earlier, negative conditioning. Coping successfully doesn't mean not feeling any stress or anxiety. It means using your coping skills, your ABCS, to stay in the situation until your commitment to face the fear has been realized. Your commitment needs to be based on your voluntary choice. The B, for breathing and relaxing, and S, for staying with it, deal with this past conditioning, which is also a cause of continuing anxiety. By being willing to seek out new opportunities to face your fears, and by using your coping skills in

---

4   As outlined by LeDoux (1996).

these situations, you can actually change your conditioning for the better and begin to remove this cause of your continuing anxiety.

These coping skills emphasize accepting and facing core fears. This is often a difficult message to hear. Many people don't want to even talk about their core fears, much less begin to face them. The reason why is that even talking about it may trigger that very anxiety or fear. However, the fact that you are reading this book means that you have the courage to begin to face your fears and anxiety. That is the first step in beginning to cope with them. A brief summary of the ABCS follows. The remaining chapters explore each point in full and offer exercises so you can practice using the ABCS to seek out and face feared situations in a way that will allow you to really make progress.

The ABCS

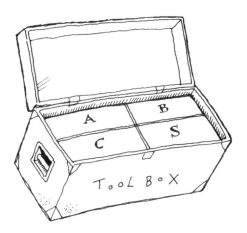

A is for acceptance of all things you cannot control. Our human nature doesn't allow us to control our emotions and the automatic thoughts (or memories) that sometimes pop into our minds. Our human nature also does not allow us to control what others think or do, or protect ourselves, or our loved ones, from all harm. We must accept the uncertainty and risk that is part of life. We may have some influence over some aspects, but we do not have complete control. So, in particular, don't get mad at yourself for feeling anxious or having other bad feelings. Acceptance means letting go of things you cannot control so you can focus on things you can do something about, like what you do and say, and what choices you make in the present moment. So once you have done your best to provide a positive influence in a given situation, you need to learn to let it go. If you have a good understanding of human nature you also know that choosing to voluntarily face unrealistic fears is the best way to reduce them (just as getting more active and productive and reaching out to those who care about you are some of the best ways to improve your mood).

B is for breathing slowly and naturally while you relax your muscle tension. High levels of anxiety or panic often trigger rapid, shallow breathing (i.e., hyperventilation). Rapid, shallow breathing increases stress by reducing the amount of carbon dioxide in your blood so much that you feel lightheaded. So, when you get anxious, choose to breathe in a slow and natural manner, drawing the breath right down into your diaphragm, and make sure you breathe out for as long as you breathe in. This will provide a positive influence on how you are feeling.

C is for countering any unrealistic or catastrophic thoughts with the truth. Look through the unrealistic thoughts and the counters that follow and circle the ones that are important for you. For example, "I can't stand feeling like this!" can be countered with: "I am learning to cope with these feelings." "I shouldn't feel anxious!" can be countered with: "I need to accept that my emotions are not under my direct control." "I shouldn't have a thought like this!" can be countered with: "This is an automatic thought and thoughts are not the same as actions." "Other people will judge me and think I am an idiot!" can be countered with: "I cannot control or even know what others think of me so I need to do what I think is right and then let it go." "I can't stand it when this memory pops into my mind!" can be countered with: "I can't block out all memories, but a memory is not the same as being there." Countering unrealistic thoughts with thoughts based on evidence and logic can have a positive influence on how you feel.

S is for staying with it so you can fully face your unrealistic fears and anxieties until they are reduced. It means not escaping or avoiding the situation, or seeking temporary relief, for example by using alcohol or drugs, or repeatedly checking for reassurance. It means fully being there as you voluntarily choose to face the fear. However, you don't have to face all your fears at once. You can take them on in a step-by-step manner. But once you have picked a feared situation to face, stay with it until you have finished your commitment.

Using coping skills such as the ABCS to face your fears is the best way that I know of to make real gains with an anxiety disorder or a problem involving disruptive anxiety and stress. It is not an easy road. There will be many ups and downs as you work toward greater independence. There are no easy shortcuts. Part of the work is to learn to be resilient after setbacks. Without experiencing setbacks you can't learn the critical lesson of resiliency. I also believe it is often necessary to develop a step-by-step plan to face your fears. The plan may be formal (written down) or more informal (just in your head or as a few notes). Either way, taking the time to develop your own plan can keep you headed in the right direction. Remember, your goal should not be to avoid all anxiety, but to function with more freedom as you work toward your other goals in life. Please keep these ideas in mind as you read the book.

Anxiety support groups, group therapy, self-help books and organizational web sites such as the one operated by the Anxiety and Depression Association of America (ADAA) are also good ways to get additional help: details can be found in the resources list at the back of the book. The ADAA web site (www.adaa.org) maintains screening tools that allow users to learn more about the type of anxiety that they may be experiencing. There is also a screening tool for depression.[5]

Reputable, educational web sites such as the one maintained by ADAA often have find-a-therapist locators to aid you in finding a local therapist, since no handbook can hope to be as effective as working directly with a well-trained psychologist or therapist who is experienced in the use of CBT. I would encourage you to seek help from an appropriately qualified professional whenever you feel you need it.

You have my permission to make copies of all the exercises, plans and forms in this book for your personal and non-commercial use. As I tell all my patients, I think it is admirable that you are willing to work on your issues with anxiety. Not everyone has the courage to do that. I hope that this book can be a part of your positive change efforts. Good luck!

---

5   These screening tools are found in the "Live and Thrive" section of the web site. However, it is best not to rely solely on self-diagnosis and self-treatment: you should visit a mental health professional for a formal diagnosis and treatment plan if you have never had your anxiety properly assessed.

Chapter 1

A IS FOR ACCEPTANCE

"Happiness and freedom begin with a clear understanding of one principle: Some things are within our control, and some things are not. It is only after you have faced up to this fundamental rule and learned to distinguish between what you can and can't control that inner tranquility and outer effectiveness become possible."

EPICTETUS, THE ART OF LIVING

"God, give us grace to accept with serenity the things that cannot be changed, courage to change the things that should be changed, and the wisdom to distinguish the one from the other."

REINHOLD NIEBUHR, THE SERENITY PRAYER

The two quotes above show that people have been thinking about dealing with stress, worry and anxiety for a very long time. In fact, some of these historic ideas have been incorporated into modern, good mental health practices. As a child, Epictetus was taken to Rome as a slave, but was later freed and because of his brilliance went on to found his own school of philosophy. He lived in perilous times and many of his writings are focused on coping with things not in one's control, while still living a virtuous life. Reinhold Niebuhr was a minister, theologian and public lecturer. It is widely believed that he wrote the Serenity Prayer in the early 1940s, while the whole world was under threat during the Second World War. His writing helps us to realize we can deal with great adversity that is outside our control, but still make a difference to that which is under our control. Niebuhr's prayer asks God for help in finding the courage to face and change that which is under our control and the ability to accept what is not in our control. Whether you pray or not, it is critical to work on these two life tasks: (1) letting go of what you can't control and (2) facing up to and taking charge of what you can control.

Both Niebuhr and Epictetus knew that serenity or peace comes from coping well with both aspects of control. From their writings we learn that, since human beings cannot dictate what other people do or think, we need to stop obsessing about it and just accept our lack of control. Sometimes we can have influence over others, but we have no real control. If we accept that we have no control then we also concede that we have no responsibility, other than the responsibility of trying to provide a positive influence. We need to let go of worries that are based on the assumption that we can control others, even if to save them from their own actions. Given that it is very difficult to accept that we often cannot rescue those we care about from their problems, it is even more difficult to accept that we do not even have complete control over aspects of our own selves!

Which Aspects of Yourself Are Actually Within Your Control?

When I use the term "control" to apply to a situation, I mean there is a singular, causal relationship between what you do and what happens. In other words, acting alone, you can bring about a given outcome. However, just as we cannot control every situation, we now understand that there are parts of ourselves that we cannot control. For example, human beings cannot control their inner feelings and emotions (even though some people are better at hiding them than others). Even those people who don't show their feelings still experience them inside. We cannot simply choose to stop all upsetting emotions. These emotions are a part of us. Although we cannot control our emotions we can influence them through our thoughts and our actions concerning the situation. However, influence is a much weaker thing than control. It means that you can help determine the outcome, but only alongside other factors. An example of influence is when you cast your vote in an election or when you speak up in a group to recommend going to a particular movie.

Even something as basic as our own cognitions (thoughts, impressions, memories, mental images, etc.) are really not under our complete, conscious control. We need to accept that we cannot control every single thought and impression that passes through our brains in a day – much less every day. The brain is a very busy place with millions of fleeting thoughts passing through it continually. Many of these thoughts are not consciously chosen. In fact, our worries, obsessions and traumatic memories are usually the very last things we would like to think about and yet we continue to do so! One simple reason why we have these very unpleasant thoughts is because we do not have complete control over these types of cognitions.

Many of our thoughts and feelings are the result of past conditioning experiences. Fear conditioning works through association. For example, if a woman is raped by a man wearing a particular cologne, even decades later if the woman smells that cologne (or one like it) it may trigger terrible memories and images of the attack along with the emotional responses that accompany the recollection. This is the result of fear conditioning, not the conscious choice of the woman. The process of fear conditioning works frequently in all of us, to trigger countless thoughts, memories and stressful emotions in everyday life, which hopefully will not always be as traumatic as the example I have used to illustrate the point.

Although we do not have control over every thought, memory or impression that gets triggered in our brains, we are able to take charge of our mental processes. An obvious example is when we focus our attention in order to complete a task (e.g., read a book, solve a math problem, hold a conversation, etc.). It follows that, since we can choose to take charge when we need to accomplish a task, we can also choose to counteract (or counter) unhealthy and unrealistic thoughts that pop into our minds. If we do this frequently we can exert a positive influence on our moods and attitudes. However, we do need to accept that it is impossible to simply choose to stop these unpleasant thoughts, memories, images and feelings from occurring in the first place. We can only choose how we react to these mental processes.

In addition to our emotions and our automatic thoughts there are many other aspects of our biology that we cannot completely control. For example, we cannot regulate the rate at which our hearts beat or control the secretion of hormones into the bloodstream. We cannot have complete control over our sexual arousal. And of course when we have insomnia, we cannot make ourselves fall asleep at our given bedtime, no matter how hard we try. We may have some influence over these parts of ourselves, but not real control. This is something we must accept if we want our sense of responsibility to match objective reality.

A Thought Experiment

Let's illustrate the importance of the concepts of acceptance, control and influence in learning to deal with anxiety with a "thought experiment." Imagine that your loved ones have been kidnapped by some very strange kidnappers. Let's assume that you know that contacting anyone, including the FBI, would not help. Let's also assume that these kidnappers will actually follow through with their threats. Finally, let's assume that you are in good health. The kidnappers have contacted you and made their bizarre demand. They insist that if you go out into the countryside, to a particular location, and dig a trench one foot deep and 100 yards long, they will release your loved ones unharmed. They also tell you that you must only use hand tools to dig, you must dig unaided and that you cannot tell anyone. The kidnappers give you two weeks to complete your task. Would you do it?

Of course you would! I have posed this thought experiment to hundreds of people and all but one said that they would dig the trench. Even though most people would find the task to be extremely difficult, almost everyone agrees that they would complete the task to release their loved ones. You would probably have blisters all over your hands from so much digging. Your hands might be bleeding and your back might be hurting before you were done. But faced with the potential outcome almost everyone would dig the trench and release their loved ones. Digging the trench is an example of something that is in your control. You choose to do it. The only sorts of things that might stop you would be very rare events which threaten your physical ability to carry out the task, such as being hit by a drunk driver on your way to dig the trench. "Control" means that there is a one-to-one relationship between what you do and what happens. You – barring freak accidents, physical injury or death – while acting alone, make it happen. You choose to go out every day and dig and your effort results in a trench 100 yards long and one foot deep. Even though this is very hard to do, you can do it if the consequence is very important to you.

Some things that fall within our control are easy and some things are hard, but if you have the control you can get it done. On the other hand, if these kidnappers had demanded that you get an ordinance passed by your local city council to ban smoking in all public spaces, you would find that a much more complex thing to achieve. Let's assume that the kidnappers have told you that you couldn't tell anyone the real reason you were trying to get the anti-smoking ordinance passed and that you would have 60 days to get it done. Faced with this demand, you could spend all your money on billboards and flyers promoting passage of the smoking ban. You could call members of the city council. You could attend city council meetings to urge the council members to support your plan. You could do all these things and more, but even so the chances that the city council would vote your way would not be very high. Many other factors beyond your control would also affect the outcome. You might be able to have some influence, but you certainly could not guarantee a positive outcome within 60 days, no matter how hard you tried. So, when you have influence you can do your best, but you need to keep in mind that other factors, that are beyond your control, are also at play. In some situations you may have a lot of influence and in others only a very small amount. Parents have a lot of influence over their young children, but it is important to remember that it is influence; not control. For example, no parent can guarantee that their children will not misbehave in a particular upcoming situation and, more importantly, no parent can guarantee that their children will be happy and successful as adults. Nonetheless, parents want to provide the most positive influence that they can on their children's development.

Many important things we can neither control nor influence. If we return again to the kidnapper thought experiment, we could imagine yet another different demand they have made. Let's assume they tell you that you have one month to acquire the ability to fly up into the air under your own power and that you would have to remain in the air for three minutes. The kidnappers then explain that you could study books about aerodynamics, you could go to the gym every day to build up the muscles in your arms and you could even glue feathers to yourself, but you could not use any device other than your own power: no airplanes, helicopters or jetpacks. In this case, you might as well give up or pursue some other means of freeing your loved ones because we all know you are never going to be able to fly. Even when things are very important to us there are times when we cannot control, or even influence, the outcome. We need to accept that as human beings we often cannot determine the outcome of the many things that are important to us. Instead we need to work on our ability to accept this truth. At the same time, we need to use our courage and our effort to focus on those things that we can control and the positive influence that can have.

When we are challenged by events we may feel tremendous stress. But our own automatic negative thoughts may add to this stress and undermine our ability to cope and to take action. If we can learn to react in the present moment by beginning to think in a realistic and healthy manner this will help us to choose wiser actions. In turn, our choices and our actions can provide a positive influence on others, such as our children, spouses or other loved ones. In addition, our behavior, healthy thoughts and choices can have a very large influence on the aspects of ourselves we cannot directly control: such as our emotions, our attitudes and even our sleep. Keeping a proper focus on what we can control combined with accepting what we cannot control is the most essential part of good mental health. I believe that we can create serenity when we combine real acceptance with the courage to take charge of things that can be controlled.

Summary of Human Nature: What We Can and Cannot Control

Human beings cannot control certain aspects of themselves, such as being able to block out all feelings of anxiety, anger, sadness, etc., or block out all negative thoughts or memories. Humans cannot regulate the exact amount of sleep they get, or always be focused and function without error.

Human beings often do not know, and cannot control, other people's thoughts, feelings or behavior.

Human beings must accept the uncertainty and risk that is a part of life. Our human nature does not allow us to eliminate all risk and uncertainty.

Human beings cannot change the past or control the future, but we are responsible, in the present moment, for our ability to react to a challenge by beginning to think in a healthy, realistic manner and for our own behavior and our own choices in that moment.

Human beings can learn to accept their human nature and can come to understand that the best way to influence (and reduce) unrealistic fears is to voluntarily face them. The best way to improve related depressed mood is to get active and productive and to make contact with others who care about us. Maintaining a healthy, realistic attitude enhances our ability to have a positive influence on our fears and mood.

Human beings can learn and change and can exert a positive influence on the things that matter most in life: our own physical and emotional health, our relationships and our future.

Control, Influence or No Influence?

We need to bring our expectations of what we can control into alignment with our human nature. There are things we can control, things we have some influence over (a lot or a little) and things we can't influence. On the chart on page 20, I have placed the following list of important issues under the headings "Control," "Influence" and "No influence." Before you look at page 20, look at the list of important issues and try to mentally place each of them under the appropriate heading. After you make your decisions, see how they compare to mine.

Important Issues

My behavior (my actions, what I do and say)

My choices (my decisions)

My healthy thoughts (thinking that is realistic and kind to me)

My automatic thoughts (thoughts that "pop into my mind")

My emotions (fear, anger, surprise, sadness, happiness, etc.)

My past (what has happened to me in the past)

My family relationships

How my children turn out (What will my children be like when they are grown-up?)

What others think of me

What others do

My health

My future

Control	Influence	No influence
My behavior	My automatic thoughts	My past
My choices	My emotions	
My healthy thoughts	My family relationships	
	How my children turn out	
	What others think of me	
	What others do	
	My health	
	My future	

"My behavior" and "my choices" are in the left-hand column of the chart under "control" as they are things that we are responsible for controlling. "My healthy thoughts" is also in this column since this refers to our ability to learn to react to stressful, automatic thoughts, such as "I can't deal with this," or "This is hopeless," with healthy and more realistic thoughts that are based on evidence or logic. For example, "This is challenging, but I can cope with it."

In the middle of the chart are the many things that we do not control, but can influence. "Automatic thoughts" are the thoughts, impressions, memories and worries that sometimes occur to us even though we don't choose them. We may learn to have some influence over our automatic thoughts. We can also learn to have some influence over our "emotions," especially if we learn and use coping skills. We can sometimes have some influence over "what others do," especially those we know best. Of course we can have some influence over "family relationships" and "how my children turn out." Finally, "my future" is also in the middle column because there is nothing we can control in the present that will guarantee an exact future. Take some time and look at each item and think about it in relation to where it is located on the chart. This may help you to gain some perspective on your important issues. The exercise at the end of this chapter will help you to begin to apply acceptance of what you can and cannot control to your own life.

Of course, the "influence" column in the middle contains items where our influence may be strong or weak. I think that only three things belong in the left-hand column of the chart: behavior, choices and healthy thoughts (i.e., the things we can control). It is important to remember that even those things on the left, that we are responsible for, are almost never done perfectly, without any error. A gymnast patient once asked me if I really thought that a perfect performance in the Olympics would be in her control. I explained that practicing diligently was in her control, but the perfect performance was something that she could only influence. You can use the chart to help you place each of your issues, then you will know if you need to work on controlling it better; or if you need to work on accepting your lack of control.

One other important point to note is that before we can exert a positive influence on anything in the middle of the chart, we must first control the three things on the left side of it: i.e., our behavior, choices and healthy thoughts, which we do by learning to counteract automatic, negative thoughts. You can learn much more about countering in Chapter 3.

Levels of Acceptance

Acceptance is one of the most important and difficult skills one can hope to master in learning to cope with anxiety. What is acceptance? It means letting go of any sense of false control we think we have and looking at ourselves and at the situation we find ourselves in as objectively as possible. It requires us to bring our thoughts and attitudes in line with a realistic appraisal of human nature and for us to accept the many things we cannot actually control. But, acceptance has many levels, ranging from emerging to a deep and comprehensive acceptance.

On the first level, you can learn how to accept the discomfort that accompanies anxiety. Typical symptoms include shakiness, rapid heartbeat or palpitations, stomach distress, sweating, dizziness, as well as numerous other unusual bodily sensations. You can learn to raise your tolerance of discomfort to a higher level in order not to obsess about these sensations. In CBT this is accomplished by changing the interpretation of these sensations from "catastrophic" to "unpleasant" and at the same time beginning to "act as if" you accept your emotions, by ceasing to avoid situations that produce anxiety and stress. As you know we can control our behavior and choose to use countering.

The second level of acceptance is even broader and more personal. It requires you to learn to accept yourself in a very realistic way. If you are a person who has anxiety, it does no good to berate yourself over this fact. Anxiety is nothing to be ashamed of or to feel guilty about since human beings do not have direct control over their emotions. You do not have to keep it a big secret or hide it from the world. Even if others say rude things about your anxiety symptoms, that is their problem and their mistake. You have done nothing wrong.

The deepest level of acceptance is a consequence of long-term progress. It will happen when you have a long track record of using the coping skills and making and fulfilling your own commitments to face your fears. When you have done this for a while, you will no longer care as much if you do feel anxiety. You will no longer evaluate yourself based on how anxious you were in a particular situation. You will evaluate yourself based on whether you accomplished the realistic goals you set and whether you have made real progress in acting in a way that is consistent with what you value in life. This deep level of acceptance will occur once you have mastered the ABCS and have made good progress with facing your fears in a step-by-step manner.

At this advanced stage you will no longer be so concerned about feeling symptoms of anxiety, but simply do whatever you commit to do, as if you had no anxiety. Making and fulfilling your own personal commitments is the essence of the S in the ABCS: the "staying with it" coping skill. Staying with it strengthens and deepens your acceptance. The paradox of this type of deep acceptance is that when you become this accepting, you rarely experience such strong symptoms of anxiety. As you go deeper into acceptance you will begin to realize that you are increasingly free of any restrictions you used to impose on yourself. Ask yourself whether you would do a certain activity or put yourself in a given situation if you did not have anxiety. Then if the answer is "yes," you can do it, in spite of the anxiety. This is the ultimate acceptance and it frees you from any limitations that you feel your anxiety disorder has placed upon you.

Over the course of your work to heal from anxiety, you will need to learn to accept all things that are not under your direct, conscious control – including what other people think and what they do (even those you care deeply about) – and accept the fact that automatic and unhealthy thoughts can pop into your mind in an instant and that trauma memories can be triggered and also return in a moment. We can't block out or erase all these kinds of thoughts, memories and emotions. What we can do is learn to accept that they can occur without our control and then react to it in a healthy manner. In recent years the importance of acceptance in coping with anxiety has received much more attention from psychologists. If you want to find out more, see, for example, Eifert and Forsyth (2005). In my view, the more we learn to accept the less we will need to counter. Of all the coping skills, acceptance pays the largest dividends in the long run.

Over the years, many patients have said, "I know I need to learn to let go, but how can I actually develop more acceptance?" The following exercise is one way in which you can learn to do this.

Exercise

Create a blank chart like the one on page 20. Using the same headings: "control," "influence" and "no influence," write out the things that upset you the most about your own anxiety problem and place each item under the appropriate heading. For example if you write: "Other people judging me negatively" that would have to go under "influence" or "no influence." If you write: "Feeling anxious and scared" that would have to go under "influence" and definitely not under "control," since none of us can fully control how we feel. Finally if you write: "Not being able to face my fear" that needs to go under "control," since finding a way to face the fear, in a step-by-step manner, is necessary in order to get better, and your behavior is under your control. Think about all the things that you need to learn to accept and all the things that you can control to a greater extent than you currently do.

One last thing: when you have finished writing out all the aspects of your anxiety that are most upsetting and have placed them under the correct headings, finally write: "Learning and using coping skills like the ABCS." Under what heading will you place this item?

Of course you can learn to use the ABCS. This is under your control.

Chapter 2

B IS FOR BREATHING AND RELAXING

"It is important to remember that there is not a single method that is unique in eliciting the Relaxation Response … One should not use the Relaxation Response in an effort to shield oneself or to withdraw from the pressures of the outside world …"

DR. HERBERT BENSON, *THE RELAXATION RESPONSE*

Breathing slowly and relaxing muscle tension is an essential part of coping with anxiety and stress. Although it is not possible to just "take control" and "will away" anxiety, it is possible to influence how you feel by taking control of your breathing and your muscle tension. Anxious breathing is very rapid and shallow. It is accompanied by large increases in muscle tension. These effects are a part of the fight or flight (or freeze) response that is the body's way of reacting to a "dangerous" situation. As outlined in the introduction, the problem with anxiety is that this response is repeatedly triggered by situations that do not actually involve physical danger. It is like a false alarm that keeps going off and causing harmful effects. Experiencing prolonged anxious breathing and lots of muscle tension can cause other symptoms of anxiety, like lightheadedness and trembling. Consciously choosing to breathe slowly and naturally and to relax excessive muscle tension can help to calm down the fight or flight (or freeze) response and help you cope more effectively. This type of slow and natural breathing is sometimes called diaphragmatic breathing. The essential feature is that it is slow and natural. It does not require extra effort. If you have ever watched someone sleeping peacefully you know what brief relaxation looks like. For most people it means taking four to six seconds to breathe in and the same amount of time to breathe out, and keeping this up for several minutes. Each breath out is accompanied by the release of more muscle tension.

Please note: there are a few medical conditions, such as advanced Parkinson's, which interfere with taking conscious control of breathing and relaxing. If this applies to you, you may have to rely more on the other anxiety coping skills.

Over the years, different methods have been developed that help prevent harmful, chronic stress. Meditation, prayers of acceptance, progressive muscle relaxation, relaxation with positive imagery, massage therapy, yoga, tai chi and other similar activities can help in this regard. These approaches are all capable of calming the body and the mind while they are being used. This can also help to break up long periods of muscle tension and anxious breathing that might otherwise last all day (or even longer). These activities can help in two ways:

1. Physically – they produce slow, natural breathing and relax muscle tension.

2. Mentally – sometimes they can help to temporarily let go of anxious thoughts.

I recommend engaging in one of these healthy activities on a regular basis to help with an anxiety or stress problem. These methods do have limitations, but are well worth pursuing. They typically take 20 to 30 minutes to do. Some of these methods may be delivered in a group setting or require going to a special class or paying for an instructor or therapist. However, this can be seen as an investment in your own well-being and you can learn the skills needed to practice on your own. Even though these more lengthy methods of relaxation are very useful holistically, in the moment when you are confronting your fear, you need a more instantaneous option. Therefore, it is imperative to have a briefer alternative available to use at a moment's notice, throughout each day, whenever you face a fear and stress rises to an uncomfortable level.

In my approach, breathing and relaxing is the B in the ABCS.[1] The ABCS are tools which can be used briefly, whenever needed throughout the day. Instructions for practicing and using the breathing technique follow. You may want to record yourself reading these instructions so you can use it for practice purposes. Pause for a few seconds any time you see an ellipsis (...) before continuing on with the text. Eventually this will become so familiar that you will be able to do it without using a recording, so you can use it at any time and in any place.

Instructions for Breathing and Relaxing

If possible, find a quiet place. Remove any gum or candy from your mouth. Sit with your legs uncrossed or recline in a comfortable chair.

Take a long, slow breath in through your nose ... Hold the breath as you slightly tense your muscles throughout your body ... and now slowly breathe out through your lips ... As you breathe out let your excessive muscle tension go ... Notice how that feels ... Now, continue to breathe in a slow and rhythmic manner without any tensing ... in through your nose ... and out through your lips ... Breathe from your stomach not from your chest ... Breathe in for four to six seconds and breathe out for four to six seconds ... Each time you breathe out let go of more and more muscle tension ... from your neck ... your shoulders ... and from throughout your whole body ... If you feel extra tension anywhere in your body – when you breathe out, let it go ... Let your breathing match the way a child breathes when they are sleeping peacefully ... Continue to breathe slowly and naturally ... Let your body

---

1   Dr. Herbert Benson wrote about a briefer technique in *The Relaxation Response* (1975). The instructions for breathing and relaxing that I use borrow from his ideas as well as from earlier ideas that appeared in *Progressive Relaxation* by Jacobson (1938).

and brain receive the message that you are safe and not in physical danger ... Each time you breathe in think the word "let" ... and when you breathe out think the word "go" ... let go of your breath ... let go of your muscle tension ... and let go of things you cannot control ... If your thoughts wander just gently return again and again to the words "let" ... and ... "go" as you breathe in and out ... Continue to breathe in this slow, rhythmic manner for several minutes ... Focus your attention on how it feels to breathe in this relaxed manner ... Focus your attention on how it feels to release excessive tension from your muscles ... Focus your thoughts on letting go of things you cannot control ... Continue to breathe slowly and naturally ... and continue to think the words "let ... go."

After a few minutes of focusing on your breathing it is time to continue on with your normal activities. But even as you do, remember to breathe in this slow and relaxed manner and remember to release extra muscle tension. This brief relaxation can be used in many situations throughout the day. You can use it as you are approaching a stressful situation and in the middle of one. You can also use it after the event to help you let it go. If you are in a private space, you can sit down and close your eyes as you practice your breathing. However, even if you are in a public space you can still get many of the benefits by using the technique without closing your eyes. You can use the technique while lying down – to help you relax before falling asleep. It can even be done while standing. Make it a habit to use the technique whenever you notice stress or excessive tension in your body.

Breathing and relaxing is the second step of the ABCS. Before you begin, remember to first accept how you feel. After you breathe and relax try countering any unrealistic thoughts that might be adding to your stress. Finally, if you are in a situation that is triggering your anxiety, stay with it until you complete the activity or until you feel more relaxed. Draw on these tools whenever you need to throughout the day.

Progressive Muscle Relaxation

At times, you may want to use one of the lengthier relaxation methods I mentioned previously, such as progressive muscle relaxation. The longer version may help you get better at relaxing so you can become more effective at using breathing for brief relaxation throughout the day. This kind of practice is usually helpful. The long version may also prove helpful for falling asleep at night.

When practicing progressive muscle relaxation, remove any candy or gum from your mouth and get into a comfortable position in a recliner or on a bed. Follow the instructions for breathing and relaxing, including the aspects about continuous, slow and natural breathing. Tense then release your muscles as instructed, except this time focus on one area of your body at a time. (As you practice any of these techniques, don't tense your muscles so much that you cause yourself any pain.)

Start with your neck and shoulders.

Then arms and hands and fingers.

Then back to neck and shoulders.

Then down to your chest and back.

Then stomach and hips.

Then your thighs.

Then down to lower legs, feet and toes.

And then back to neck and shoulders.

Then finally, up to muscles around your jaw, eyes and mouth.

As you work through these areas of the body, breathe in as you tense the muscles for a few seconds. Then as you breathe out, release all the muscle tension in that area. Continue to breathe in this slow and natural manner and continue to relax the muscles until you are ready to move on to the next muscle group. You only need to tense the muscles once at the beginning of your focus on that area. However, if one part of your body is more difficult to relax you can repeat the tensing and releasing process several times. I often focus more on the neck and shoulders because that is a very common site of extra muscle tension.

Exercise

Use the instructions above to practice breathing for brief relaxation once a day, thinking "let" as you breathe in and then "go" as you breathe out. This kind of daily practice will improve your brief relaxation skills and may also benefit your general emotional and physical health. Use brief relaxation techniques whenever you face higher levels of anxiety and begin to incorporate breathing and relaxing whenever you need it throughout the day. If you have problems falling asleep, use brief relaxation or progressive muscle relaxation techniques to help get you ready for sleep. You could continue to use a longer relaxation exercise, such as progressive muscle relaxation, on a weekly basis (or more often if that is helpful to you).

It is important to practice breathing and relaxation exercises until you can reliably and effectively use this aspect of the ABCs to help you cope with stress and anxiety. But remember that using breathing for brief relaxation is not running away from fear; it is to help you face your fear.

Chapter 3

C IS FOR COUNTERING

"It is important to learn how to think clearly … Name the situation as it is; don't filter it through your judgments."

EPICTETUS, *THE ART OF LIVING*

Countering means responding to and replacing unrealistic and unhealthy thoughts with new thoughts that are based on evidence and logic. The old, automatic thoughts are usually based on jumps to conclusions with little basis in evidence or logic. Although it is not possible to control every single thought that passes through our brains, it is possible to learn to question and then counter unrealistic, unhealthy thoughts and that can be extremely important in the recovery process. Most unhealthy, unrealistic thoughts seem to be first learned in childhood, adolescence or certainly by young adulthood. It is particularly important to realize that not every thought or belief you learned during these formative times is true or helpful.

As children, we learn from our interactions with parents, siblings and others. We learn from our direct experiences and we learn vicariously, from our observations of others in real life and also through stories and other media. We develop thoughts about ourselves and about our interactions with others. Even in families that actively try to foster a healthy self-confidence in their children, it is still possible for a child to learn or internalize thoughts that are not accurate and not helpful. Some of these unrealistic, unhealthy thoughts can contribute to anxiety (e.g., "I'm an idiot," or "I can't handle this like other people can," or "I can't let the family down by making a mistake in public," or "It would be horrible if someone got angry at me."). In families where the adults are less aware of the effects this kind of thinking can have, it is even easier for a child to learn unhealthy and unrealistic thoughts.

Even after many years, negative thoughts that were established in childhood and adolescence often occur at times of challenge, when we are trying to deal with a difficult situation. The thoughts may occur again and again and the brain may go from one unhealthy thought to another for minutes, or hours, at a time. The more these thoughts are believed and the more often they occur, the more stress is produced. It can become a vicious circle because as more stress is produced it is easier for the brain to produce more of these unrealistic, unhealthy thoughts. So around and around we go, producing more and more stress.

Recurrent unhealthy thoughts are not based on sound evidence or logical thinking. Since we first learn to think about ourselves and about others when we are children, it should be no surprise that this is the case. When we are children our ability to base our thinking on solid evidence and logic is not as evolved. A child's brain doesn't discriminate between realistic and unrealistic thoughts. By the time a child is a teen, these types of thoughts may have become very well learned. The thoughts may contain deeply held assumptions that are never questioned and are simply the way the individual sees their place in the world. As adults, we can learn to question and counter negative, unrealistic thoughts. But first we have to become aware of them.

Types of Automatic, Unhealthy and Unrealistic Thinking

There are two basic types of unhealthy, unrealistic thinking that frequently occur with, and cause, the stressful emotions which can lead to self-defeating behaviors.[1] You may recognize these types of automatic thoughts from emotionally troubled times in childhood and adolescence as this is often when they are first learned. The two basic types are jumping to conclusions (based on little or no evidence) and misplaced responsibilities. You may jump to conclusions about a variety of different things including yourself, other people's worth, other people's thoughts and feelings and the future. Misplaced responsibilities involve denying your human nature by: (1) not taking responsibility for things you can actually control and do something about or (2) trying to control things that cannot really be controlled. Automatic thoughts are not based on solid evidence or logic.

Exercise

Read through the following list that includes several examples of jumping to conclusions and misplaced responsibilities. Place two ticks next to each example of unhealthy and unrealistic thinking that you do frequently. Place one tick beside those that you do occasionally.

---

1   Many psychologists including A. Ellis and R.A. Harper (1961), A.T. Beck et al. (1979) and D.D. Burns (1980) have developed different ways of categorizing unrealistic, unhealthy thoughts. These works are listed in the bibliography, should you wish to find out more.

Types of Automatic Thoughts

1. Jumping to conclusions.

    a. Jumping to conclusions about yourself: "I can't do anything right." "I am a fool." "I am a stupid loser." ☐☐

    b. Jumping to conclusions about others: "She is a complete fool." "He is pathological." "He is an S.O.B." ☐☐

    c. Jumping to conclusions about others' thoughts and feelings: "He hates me." "She thinks I am a wimp." "Everyone is mad at me." ☐☐

    d. Jumping to conclusions about the future: "I know I will have a miserable time at the party." "My relationship will end badly." "My family will all die in a car crash." "I will be fired." "Someone will break in and kill us." ☐☐

2. Misplaced responsibilities.

    a. Avoiding responsibility for things that are in your control: "When I feel that way I just can't leave the house." "She makes me so upset that I have to hit her." "When I feel anxious I have to leave." "I cannot change." "When I feel stress I must do anything to stop it." ☐☐

    b. Taking responsibility for things that are not in your control: "I shouldn't be anxious." "I can't make mistakes in front of others." "It is my fault he raped me." "I shouldn't feel this way." "I should be able to block out bad memories and worries." "I should be able to protect my loved ones from harm." ☐☐

People with anxiety or depression usually report being troubled by some of these types of unhealthy, unrealistic thinking, so if you recognize this in yourself, you are not alone. However, as you now know it is important to begin to question and counter these thoughts when they occur. At the end of this chapter I have included a copy of a blank incident log that you can copy and use to organize your thoughts and feelings around particular situations you find upsetting. You can use the log to identify the unhealthy, unrealistic thoughts that crop up when you are in stressful situations. Then you can counter those particular thoughts on the log sheet. If you use the log sheet several times you will probably discover that, whatever the situation that triggers your anxiety, the same patterns of unrealistic thoughts repeat themselves over and over again. Some or all of your stream of automatic thoughts may need to be countered.

A copy of a sample incident log follows. This shows how to record, in just a few factual words, the situation, your emotions in the situation and your automatic thoughts. This sample illustrates how to use the downward arrow technique to get deeper and deeper into your thoughts and the core fears that were triggered by the distressing situation. Remember, your automatic thoughts may not be an error. If that is the case, write N/A in that box, as shown in the sample log.

Sample Incident Log

Date	Situation	Feelings
April 16	Got parking ticket	Anxious

Automatic Thoughts	Type of Error	Healthy Response
"This is annoying." ↓	Not applicable (N/A)	N/A
"I always do this!" ↓	Jumping to conclusions	"I have not had a ticket in months."
"I am stupid." ↓	Jumping to conclusions	"Making a mistake doesn't mean I'm stupid."
"I should never make mistakes." ↓	Misplaced responsibility	"Humans make mistakes!"
"When I feel stress I can just go home without finishing my errands."	Misplaced responsibility	"I need to face my fear without running away."

The Downward Arrow Technique

The downward arrow technique was described by the psychiatrist David Burns in his book *Feeling Good: The New Mood Therapy* (1980). You write down the first automatic thought that occurred to you in the distressing situation, then you ask yourself probe questions to pull out the next thought in the chain (e.g., "What is so bad about this?" or "What does this mean to me?" etc.). Then you write down the next automatic thought. You continue until you have written down all your automatic thoughts. Next, you determine whether any of your automatic thoughts are unhealthy and unrealistic (in other words, do they involve jumping to conclusions or misplaced responsibility?). If so, you note the type of error and counter the unhealthy, unrealistic thought. Focus first and foremost on countering the thoughts that upset you the most. If you are working with a psychologist it would be very helpful to share your written records with that person. As mentioned, a blank incident log can be found at the end of this chapter to help you record this.

Whatever the exact content of your automatic thoughts, if they are examples of unhealthy and unrealistic thinking, then they need to be countered. Remember that these thoughts are just examples of old, faulty learning. Remind yourself that the thoughts that pop into your head when you are anxious or depressed are often not true: this is itself a good counter.

Of course, we may face some situations which are extremely challenging. If our thoughts in these instances are realistic, then we need to face and accept the difficult situation. We should not use countering to try to convince ourselves that nothing is wrong if we are actually facing a difficulty that is beyond our control. Only unrealistic thoughts need to be countered. For example, you might have recurrent thoughts about your job security. If you have no evidence to suggest there is a problem, these thoughts may be unrealistic. However, if your boss has expressed concern about the company's future, and has said that some jobs may be lost, you would need to accept and prepare for this potentially very difficult situation, which I am sure you would want to do. Most people prefer to know about an upcoming problem rather than being caught by surprise – with no time to prepare and little time to practice using coping skills.

In order to give you a head start in countering those typical unhealthy thoughts that lead to more anxiety I have provided examples that commonly occur with different anxiety disorders. I have also listed the type of error and an example of a good counter. If the counters seem to fit for you, you may want to use them with your own thoughts. You may want to circle the ones that apply to you. If the automatic thought does not apply to you then skip to the next one.

Key Counters for Specific Anxiety Disorders

Social Anxiety

1. **Automatic thought:** "It is a catastrophe if others think a negative thought about me. I can't live if others disapprove of me or notice that I am feeling anxious, so I can never speak up if there is a conflict."

    Type of error: jumping to conclusions and misplaced responsibility.

    Counter: "I need to realize that my automatic thoughts may not be true. I often can't know and can never control what others think. I cannot control my emotions. I need to accept that emotions like fear, anxiety and panic are not under my direct control. It is not a catastrophe if others think a negative thought about me or disapprove of something I do or say or feel. It is my responsibility to do what I think is right and then let it go. Sometimes I need to speak up. I can be tactful and assertive in what I say. I also need to use the ABCS to accept and cope with my social anxiety so it can reduce over time."

2. **Automatic thought:** "If others notice that my hands are shaking or my face is red or my voice is breaking, I won't be able to bear it."

   Type of error: jumping to conclusions and misplaced responsibility.

   Counter: "I don't have control over all my symptoms of stress and I need to accept that and still do what I think is right. I can't control what others think. They may not even notice these things as much as I do. I need to realize that my automatic thoughts may not be true: it won't matter if others notice my stress."

3. **Automatic thought:** "When I am performing in front of others (e.g., in sports, in speech class, on stage, at work, in a social situation, etc.), I must always avoid mistakes and act with total confidence or it is impossible for me to cope and finish the performance."

   Type of error: jumping to conclusions and misplaced responsibility.

   Counter: "I need to do my best to focus on the situation at hand and also cope with any stress that arises (e.g., by using the ABCS). Being free from all errors is not in my control. All human beings make mistakes at times. I can quickly recover from any error and not dwell on it. I can refocus on the situation, do my best and then let the rest go."

4. **Automatic thought:** "If I get too stressed in a social situation I will throw up, or get diarrhea, or embarrass myself in some other way, and that would be more than I can bear. I must avoid social situations."

   Type of error: jumping to conclusions and misplaced responsibility.

Counter: "It is extremely unlikely that I will throw up or have diarrhea right in the middle of a social situation and even if it did happen, I could cope. There are important reasons for me to participate in social situations. Escape and avoidance will only make the fear worse next time. Repetition can help me become more comfortable over time. I need to realize that my automatic thoughts may not be true. I can use the ABCS to help deal with this social situation."

Panic with Agoraphobia

1. **Automatic thought:** "I am having a heart attack, being smothered, dying or losing control of my mind: I can't stand thinking and feeling this way!"

   Type of error: jumping to conclusions and misplaced responsibility.

   Counter: "I have learned to think this way, but that doesn't make it true. My medical doctor has said that I am physically okay. It is what it is. I am feeling anxiety or panic. I need to accept that emotions and feelings like fear, anxiety and panic are not under my direct control. However, I can control how I react to them. I need to realize that my automatic thoughts may not be true. I am not dying and I can use my coping skills to cope with these feelings. I can use the ABCS to accept and cope with my panic so it can reduce over time."

2. **Automatic thought:** "When I am waiting in line in a store, or driving in busy traffic, or sitting in the middle of a large audience, I feel trapped and anxious and I can't stand feeling that way. I have to find the closest exit and go home."

   Type of error: jumping to conclusions and misplaced responsibility.

Counter: "I need to accept my feelings and then cope with them using the ABCS. It is my responsibility to learn to face my fear and not run away from it. I need to realize that my automatic thoughts may not be true."

Generalized Anxiety Disorder (GAD)

GAD refers to chronic, excessive worry. Obsessive compulsive disorder (OCD) and illness anxiety are listed separately below, but the three conditions can be very similar at times.

1. **Automatic thought:** "If my boss doesn't smile at me when I pass her in the hall that means she is about to fire me from my job. If I get fired I will probably never be able to get another job like this and I won't be able to pay my bills. I will probably lose my house and have to file for bankruptcy. Then my spouse will probably take the kids and leave me since I am such a failure. I will be depressed and all alone. I need to check several times a day to see if my job performance is okay."

   Type of error: jumping to conclusions and misplaced responsibility.

   Counter: "My boss sometimes doesn't smile when she sees other people she knows. There is no real evidence she is planning to fire me. If I ever lose my job I will find another one, even if I have to move or take a position with lower pay. My spouse loves me and I have no evidence that my marriage will be wrecked if I lose this job. I need to work hard in my role, but then accept that I can't control everything. I need to stop asking my boss for feedback so often. My checking doesn't make my job safer, but can make my boss upset with me. I need to accept the uncertainty and risk that are a part of life. I need to use the ABCS to face and cope with these recurrent thoughts so they can reduce over time."

2. **Automatic thought:** "If I have an important task coming up in the future I need to know, right away and in detail, how I will handle every eventuality. When I am thinking about a new task, if I can't solve all the potential problems immediately then the whole thing will be a disaster."

    Type of error: jumping to conclusions and misplaced responsibility.

    Counter: "I need to accept that complicated tasks involving other people can have millions of possible permutations. No human can know exactly what will happen in the future. I can't know now whether the whole thing will be a disaster. Some disasters that I imagine will never happen. I need to have a general plan then focus on each step in turn – and let the rest go until, and if, I need to deal with a new challenge. I can't solve everything at once: I need to face one situation at a time, when I get to it. I need to use the ABCS and realize that my automatic thoughts may not be true."

Illness Anxiety

1. **Automatic thought:** "My symptoms mean I am about to die. My skin imperfection must mean I have skin cancer, my headache means I have a brain tumor, my stomach ache means I have stomach cancer and the tightness in my chest means I am having a heart attack – and I need to check to make sure I'm okay."

    Type of error: jumping to conclusions and misplaced responsibility.

    Counter: "I have learned to think this way, but that doesn't make it true. I saw my doctor about these concerns and I was told that these symptoms do not mean what I think they do: I do not have a medical problem. This is an obsession and I need to not act on it so it can weaken over time. I need to accept the uncertainty and risk that are a part of life. I need to use the ABCS to face and cope with my health obsessions and compulsions so they can reduce over time."

2. **Automatic thought:** "I must fall asleep because if I cannot sleep it means I will fall apart and not be able to function."

    Type of error: jumping to conclusions and misplaced responsibility.

    Counter: "I need to accept that no one has complete control over their sleep. If I don't fall asleep within a few minutes, I will get up and do something until I feel sleepier then give it another try. If worry is blocking sleep I may get up and make some notes about a plan for dealing with it then go back to bed. If I don't sleep well I will probably be tired, but I won't actually fall apart. I need to use the ABCS to accept and cope with the fact that my sleep patterns may vary."

OCD

Please note: the next automatic thought includes dealing with the aggressive or "deviant" thoughts that are characteristic of some types of OCD. These thoughts can cause a person with OCD to become extremely upset, even if they would never act upon them. This is a characteristic of this type of OCD: I have found that many people who suffer from this type of OCD are horrified when these thoughts pop into their minds and are extremely unlikely to actually harm others. However, if you are having thoughts about hurting others then you will need to immediately have a comprehensive evaluation by an experienced mental health professional. Please see the resources list for assistance in finding someone to do an evaluation.

1. **Automatic thought:** "If an aggressive, or sexually deviant, or immoral or blasphemous thought pops into my mind it means I will act on the thought. I need to avoid situations that might trigger these thoughts and I need to check on myself to make sure I don't act on these thoughts. I need to think enough good thoughts to make up for the bad thoughts."

   Type of error: jumping to conclusions and misplaced responsibility.

   Counter: "I need to realize that my automatic thoughts may not be true. My psychologist says that my diagnosis is OCD and this is why I have these thoughts. I need to accept that thoughts are not the same as actions and that no one can control all their thoughts. I have no history of acting on these thoughts. These are not my positive fantasies: in fact, I am horrified when these thoughts pop into my head. That is not the profile of someone who would act on these thoughts. People who act on these thoughts enjoy having the thoughts. No, I am obsessing and I need to not avoid situations or frequently check on myself, because that would only feed the obsession. I need to stop trying to make up for bad thoughts because that only feeds my obsession. My chances of acting on these types of thoughts are extremely low, but I need to accept the uncertainty and risk that are a part of life. I need to use the ABCS to face and cope with these thoughts so they can reduce over time."

2. **Automatic thought:** "If I don't maintain a perfect balance and organization then I just can't stand it. If I tap two times on one side I have to tap two times on the other. My shoes, clothes and the items on my desk have to be in exact, perfect order."

   Type of error: misplaced responsibility.

   Counter: "It may be difficult, but I can stand it if things are not in perfect order. I want to become more flexible. I need to start to break some of these rigid rules and use the ABCS so my compulsions can reduce over time."

3. **Automatic thought:** "I will forget to turn off an electrical appliance, or lock a window or door, or put away something … and that will cause a catastrophe. It will be my fault and I won't be able to stand it."

   Type of error: jumping to conclusions and misplaced responsibility.

   Counter: "Checking more than once is compulsive. I need to accept that I cannot eliminate all risk from life – even if I spent all my time checking that wouldn't eliminate risk entirely. Some risk is literally a part of life. I need to use the ABCS to accept and cope with my compulsions so they can reduce over time."

4. **Automatic thought:** "If my spouse doesn't call right away, or doesn't smile as much, or acts differently that means that I am not loved and they are about to leave me. I need to check with them or check on them to be sure that I am still loved."

   Type of error: jumping to conclusions and misplaced responsibility.

   Counter: "Checking more than once is compulsive. Checking to see if I am loved will drive away my loved one. Some risk is a part of life. I need to use the ABCS to accept and cope with this compulsion and realize that my automatic thoughts may not be true."

5. **Automatic thought:** "If I don't wash, disinfect and clean up 'contamination' frequently, or completely avoid it, then I will be contaminated. I will then contaminate others. I cannot stand feeling this way."

   Type of error: jumping to conclusions and misplaced responsibility.

Counter: "It is impossible to avoid all things that might be contaminated. Cleaning too frequently or aggressively every day is compulsive. I need to accept that I cannot eliminate all risk of contamination from life – even if I spent all my time cleaning that wouldn't eliminate the risk. Some risk is a part of life. I need to use the ABCS to accept and cope with my obsessions and compulsions so they can reduce over time."

OCD is an exception to this general use of countering. While education and correction of faulty beliefs can still be helpful, it is important not to rely too much on detailed countering. Rather, simply face the obsessive fear and label feared thoughts as an obsession. People with OCD sometimes believe that if they can counter in "just the right way" then their obsessive fears will melt away. But if you have a diagnosis of OCD, this extensive, detailed and repetitive countering can become a part of your compulsions! So, if this applies to you, focus on trying to label your obsessive thought as an obsession and try to postpone, limit and eventually end your compulsions. See Chapter 7 for more information.

Post-traumatic Stress Disorder (PTSD)

Please note: if you suffer from PTSD I urge you to seek out an experienced psychologist or mental health professional who is experienced in treating the disorder, for example a cognitive behavioral therapist who is familiar with exposure techniques. Please see the resources list for sources of more information.

Automatic thought: "I cannot stand remembering the terrible things that happened. I will be overwhelmed."

Type of error: jumping to conclusions and misplaced responsibility.

Counter: "There is no way to successfully erase these memories. The memories must be faced, by choosing to go over them in detail, time after time. It will be very upsetting when I allow myself to face all these memories, but if I use the ABCS I can tell my story to someone I trust (e.g., a cognitive behavioral therapist) and it will get easier with repetition. I need to remember the most upsetting details and not shut down or run away, so the repetitions can allow healing to occur. The good news is that I am no longer in the terrible circumstance in which the memory was made. Now I am safe."

Depressive Rumination

Please note: depression occurs very frequently with anxiety. For some people the same background factors that produce anxiety also produce episodes of depression. For others an anxiety disorder may cause so many limitations and losses in their life that it is easy to fall into depression as well. Severe depression can block effective treatment of anxiety. For these reasons, I have only included information on coping with depression that is related to anxiety. If you also suffer with depression, I encourage you to carefully review this section on depressive rumination and also read and review Chapter 5: Coping with Related Depression. If your depression blocks all progress you will need to seek help from a mental health professional. Please see the resources list for more information.

Automatic thought: "I cannot face getting up or going out. I have to avoid contact with others because I have been hurt so much and feel so bad. I will put off anything I need to do until later."

Type of error: jumping to conclusions and misplaced responsibility.

Counter: "It is human nature to become more depressed if I isolate myself, procrastinate and become inactive. I need to set healthy personal goals. Then I need to use my depression coping skills (e.g., following the Ten Rules for Coping with Depression in Chapter 5) to help me to get up, washed and dressed every day. Then I need to spend the day interspersing periods of productivity with shorter periods of relaxation or recreation. Exercise, such as a good walk, is one way to be productive. I also need to make contact with people who are supportive and be prepared to be assertive with those who are not supportive. Finally, at the end of the day, I need to write down at least one good thing that happened, no matter how small."

Exercise

I encourage you to review the sample incident log on page 38, which demonstrates how to capture your thoughts and feelings about a situation. Then use a blank incident log to sort out your thoughts and feelings following situations that you have found distressing (the template is on page 51). The incident logs provide a good way for you to practice accepting what you need to accept and countering what you need to counter. If you are working with a therapist or psychologist who is trained in CBT you may find it helpful to explore your logs with them.

Incident Log

Date	Situation	Feelings

Automatic Thoughts	Type of Error	Healthy Response

Of course, we are aiming to counter unhealthy and unrealistic thoughts at the moment they occur. But, I have found that using the log sheets is a very helpful way of learning to do this. Once you have repeatedly filled out your log sheets you will find that you are countering the same core unhealthy thoughts over and over. After a while, the countering process becomes more and more automatic. Many people have reported that they find keeping a journal is also helpful. If you keep a journal, please try to incorporate the basic ideas about countering into your entries.

The incident logs can be used in a number of different scenarios.

Use the blank incident log to explore a recent event that produced lots of anxiety. Be sure to pay lots of attention to getting all of your important automatic thoughts down on paper before you start to see which thoughts may be unhealthy and unrealistic, and therefore need to be countered. Use the downward arrow technique: when you have written down the first automatic thought that occurs to you, ask yourself "What is so bad about this?" or "What does this mean?" or "Where does this lead?" Then write down your next automatic thought. Continue on in this fashion until you have written down all these linked thoughts – including the core, most troubling thought. Now it is time to identify the thoughts that are unhealthy and unrealistic. Write down the type of error next to these thoughts. Don't forget to record a realistic counter for each of the unhealthy thoughts.

Use a blank log sheet to write up an incident that occurred in your past that was very upsetting. It is never too late to sort out your thoughts and feelings in a healthier, more realistic manner.

Use a blank log sheet to write up a future situation that you may be worrying about. You can use log sheets to help you cope with anticipatory anxiety.

After you have familiarized yourself with using log sheets you can begin to rely more on countering in the moment rather than writing down your responses. However, if an incident is especially difficult to cope with then don't hesitate to use a written incident log to help you sort your thoughts and feelings into a more realistic and healthy form. Fully incorporate countering into your use of the ABCS.

Chapter 4

S is for Staying with it

"Courage is resistance to fear, mastery of fear not absence of fear."

Mark Twain, *Pudd'nhead Wilson and Those Extraordinary Twins*

It is not possible to make progress in coping with anxiety without facing the situations that make you anxious. In the short run, facing fears will likely increase your anxiety but you will need to accept this result, and trust that you will be able to cope. In the long run, you will give yourself the opportunity to practice your coping skills. Voluntarily facing the situations that trigger anxiety, and then using your skills to cope with them, is absolutely necessary to getting better. The last of the ABCS is S for staying with it. At the most concrete level "staying with it" means fully facing the feared situation without trying to escape or distract yourself. It involves not leaving the situation until at least one of the following happens: (1) your anxiety is somewhat reduced or (2) the amount of time that you initially committed to stay with it has elapsed. If you fully face your feared situation and you stay with it until one or both of these conditions are met you will have made progress no matter how much anxiety you felt.

"Staying with it" also means following through with using your coping skills in the long term. Getting better and fully recovering from anxiety is completely possible but it can take a long time. There is no magic cure for this type of complicated problem. Even after longer periods of success and feeling much better, there will inevitably be days that are much more distressing than others, but this shouldn't cause you to lose heart. When one of those days occurs, it is critical to instead focus on bouncing back, by using coping skills like the ABCS and the Ten Rules for Coping with

Depression (described in Chapter 5). You have to get through these more distressing times in order to continue with your progress, which you have the coping skills to do. If you give up and give in by staying in bed and avoiding, then you go back to the old negative patterns. Like a road through the mountains, the road to recovery has many ups and downs, but if you continue to use your coping skills you will eventually get to your destination.

It is very important that you measure your day-to-day progress by whether you seek out opportunities to face your fears and use the ABCS – including the S. Do not use the amount of anxiety you feel as your measure of daily progress. Human beings cannot directly control their feelings and emotions. You know that if you begin to seek out situations that you have been avoiding you will probably feel more anxiety in the short run, not less. If you keep pushing the boundaries and don't allow anxiety to force you to escape or avoid those situations, then in the long run you will produce a great positive influence on your emotions. You will feel more free and you will probably also feel much less anxious. "Staying with it" means sticking with your step-by-step plan over the weeks, months and years that follow. It is like putting a small amount of money in the bank each week and collecting interest. In the long run the value will compound and after many years you will be rich.

A good way of planning to face your fears is to estimate how high your stress level might be in a particular circumstance. Once you have estimated your likely stress as "very high," "high," "moderate," "low" or "none," try to put yourself in situations that are a bit out of your comfort zone, but are not overwhelming. Those estimated "low" or "moderate" stress would be a good place to start. Try to keep experiencing those same situations over and over, until you start to get more comfortable in them by using your coping skills. Then push the boundaries again and take on the next level. It may take a long time to work your way up to "very high," but if you stick with the process then it will bring rich rewards.

You will need to fully expose yourself to each situation, without trying to escape or distract yourself. Distraction techniques vary by individual, but may include counting ceiling tiles, staring out the window, or just mentally withdrawing. Distraction often feels good in the moment, but it usually blocks progress. When patients tell me they have been facing their fears for years without getting better that usually means they have been relying too much on distraction. Often distraction is just another way to escape or to avoid facing the situation completely. Sometimes distraction can be a good thing, if it helps you to avoid negative aspects of anxiety driven behavior. If you have a plan to face your fears on a daily basis then you may use distraction to help you avoid performing compulsions, checking or worrying, as we will see in Chapter 7. The key point here is to be honest with yourself about whether you are using distraction constructively or for escapism.

If you are in a situation which seems overwhelming, take a few moments to use the ABCS and try to remain where you are. The next best option is to excuse yourself, for instance to go to the bathroom where you can practice the ABCS before returning to the situation. The next option is to make an excuse to go outside where you can take a couple of moments to regain your composure, using the ABCS, and then go back inside. If you did need to completely leave the situation and were unable to go back inside, vow to return to it later that day or at the next opportunity. Of course, this final option is the one that is most likely to block your progress.

Once you are using the ABCS to voluntarily seek out and face situations that make you uncomfortable it is important to remember that they can also be used when you have anticipatory anxiety before an upcoming event. You can accept that the situation is imminent, and at the same time breathe and relax, then counter any unrealistic thoughts and finally stay with the fact that the event is upcoming and that you are going to face it for a few moments, before you try to let it all go and get back into your present moment. You will need to be prepared to do this repeatedly.

If you find yourself ruminating in great detail over every moment of your last fear-producing situation, while beating yourself up by criticizing and condemning every little thing that you did, you will need to engage your coping skills. This type of unrealistic thinking needs to be countered. Likewise, if you review the situation and condemn yourself for feeling anxious, this is an example of misplaced responsibility that you need to counter. So after a stressful situation, be ready to use the ABCS to interrupt this unhealthy retrospective reviewing of "past failure." Condemning yourself because you felt anxious will block progress. If you voluntarily faced a situation that made you very anxious, you used courage and you deserve credit – not condemnation. You will need to remind yourself of this repeatedly in order to break this unhealthy pattern. As you continue to use your coping skills to face your fears, you can get better.

Escape Behavior

In addition to simply avoiding or exiting a fear-producing situation, some individuals engage in a wide variety of other behaviors that can temporarily diminish their anxiety and stress. This "escape" behavior that ends an aversive condition like anxiety or stress is automatically reinforced.[1] The more these behaviors occur, the more entrenched they become. If you are experiencing high levels of anxiety and stress then these behaviors may seem very tempting. However, most of these escape behaviors and associated activities are extremely detrimental in the long run. They are not examples of good coping skills. The use of these impulsive behaviors to escape or avoid anxiety and stress can lead to serious health and relationship problems.

---

1 For more information see Malott, Whaley and Malott (1997), especially pages 32–49.

Drugs

Especially troublesome is the use of drugs to escape anxiety and distress, because of the adverse effects this habitual behavior can have. Drugs of choice may be illegal or legal and include over the counter or prescription medications. Some definitions of a drug include the more socially accepted alcohol and cigarettes, or other products that contain nicotine, and excessive use of all these products can have dire health consequences. All of these substances induce an immediate emotional state that serves to calm or distract users from their distress – in the short run. Those who habitually turn to these products to control distress do not focus on learning replacement, constructive coping skills. Using alcohol or drugs to escape from anxiety, or other bad feelings, is a deadly trap because it can feel good at the time. With many of these substances, tolerance will increase and, as time goes on, it will take a higher dose to produce the same emotional effect. The long-term effects are often very negative and if the user is not able to set clear limits, then alcoholism, nicotine dependency or drug addiction is a likely outcome. We all know that chronic drug or alcohol abuse can cause serious health problems, including death. The health risks of smoking are similarly severe and well documented. However, many millions of people abuse alcohol and other drugs and many of them began this pattern in order to escape their feelings of stress and anxiety.

Chronic smoking is sometimes not seen as a detriment to emotional health, but I believe that it does present a risk since it can take the place of learning to use healthy coping skills. Although some smokers report that they experience positive emotional effects from smoking cigarettes, evidence from studies suggests that those who do successfully quit smoking experience reduced levels of depression, anxiety and stress compared to those who don't quit.[2]

2   See Taylor et al. (2014) for details.

Several decades ago I toured a residential facility for sufferers of alcohol and drug abuse. I asked the clinical director how many of those residents' problems had begun as a way to diminish their feelings of stress and anxiety. He confirmed that the majority had started abusing drugs or alcohol for just these reasons. It seems clear to me that not only are there substantial medical risks involved, but there are also long-term negative effects on emotional health when an individual uses these chemical forms of escapism. If you find yourself turning to these escape behaviors, I wholeheartedly urge you to focus on developing healthier coping mechanisms instead. It is a natural human instinct to engage in behaviors that offer us comfort, but the long-term detrimental effects make this physically and emotionally untenable.

Can Prescribed Medications Become Escape Behaviors?

I am not a medical doctor but, in my professional experience as a psychologist, I have noticed that even prescription anti-anxiety medications can sometimes become a problem for individuals with an anxiety disorder. Some anti-anxiety medications produce an immediate feeling of relaxation. These medications typically belong to a class of drugs known as benzodiazepines. Some individuals come to rely exclusively on these types of medication and give up on trying to learn and use coping skills. Because the body can develop an increased tolerance when the drugs are taken for a long time, individuals may begin to feel they need higher and higher dosages of these medications. Some even get separate prescriptions from different doctors in order to take more than should be prescribed. Some individuals may mix alcohol with these medications to get a greater effect. The result of this type of abuse is addiction.

On the other hand, anti-depressant medications are sometimes used to treat anxiety and these do not cause this type of risk. If your doctor has prescribed an anti-depressant for your anxiety disorder, you do not have to be concerned about addiction. Your doctor will be able to advise you about the best course of treatment for you; please do voice any concerns or queries you may have with them.

The underlying issue with certain anti-anxiety medications is the immediate and strong relaxing effect, an effect that typical anti-depressant medications do not produce. While this may be deemed medically necessary in the short term, we must take care that it doesn't become an addiction. If you have been prescribed one of these medications then I encourage you to discuss it with your doctor, be very careful about long-term use and never increase the dose beyond your doctor's recommendation.

Of course, many people do take anti-anxiety medications without developing an addiction. Many of my patients take an anti-anxiety medication as well as undergoing therapy. The key is that they see the need to learn and use those anxiety coping skills and hope to eventually reduce or eliminate their medication. They are reluctant to take high doses of these medications for weeks or months at a time because they understand the risks. Crucially, they do not rely on these medications as the only way to cope.

Additional Escape Behaviors

In the same way that drugs can be used to escape anxiety it is possible to excessively use behaviors like gambling, watching pornography, video gaming, shopping or eating to distract from negative feelings. Even work can serve as a distraction from the anxiety, stress or other bad feelings in our personal lives. That is why workaholism is a real phenomenon. I once worked with a patient who was extremely calm and confident in his work environment, but experienced high levels of stress in his personal life. He worked 80–100 hours a week and had little time for his wife and family. As long as this pattern of escape and avoidance continued he couldn't make much progress in his personal life.

These behaviors and activities are not necessarily unhealthy in and of themselves. For example, playing video games can be harmless entertainment and shopping, eating and working productively can certainly be positive. These questions may help to identify when these activities become a problem: (1) Does the activity occur every time extra stress is experienced and does it serve to diminish the stress in the short run? (2) Does the behavior or activity have detrimental effects on physical or emotional health or family life in the long run? If the answer is "yes," then it is likely that it is a self-defeating pattern and you are using the activity to escape, or avoid, stress and anxiety.

NOT ALL WAYS OF COPING
ARE HEALTHY

Reducing Escape Behaviors

As you can see, when you have an anxiety disorder, many different activities and substances can form the basis of self-defeating patterns. Becoming aware of a self-defeating pattern of behavior is the first step in doing something about it. The second step is to remind yourself of the detrimental long-term effects when the urge to use these distractions occurs. Your reminder needs to be strong and clear and you need to believe it (e.g., "If I continue to distract myself from my fears rather than face them, then my fears will gain more control over me."). The last step is to act on that reminder by making a better choice.

When I first saw Tim he reported a long history of social anxiety. He also suffered from related depression – which worsened whenever he experienced conflict with others. He told me that when this had happened recently, he had resorted to going to the bar "to get plastered." He also reported that he had started to have a few drinks before social outings so he would feel more relaxed. As a part of his treatment, Tim began to set clear limits on his use of alcohol. There were ups and downs in his progress, but he eventually stopped his progression into alcoholism and we were able to successfully complete his treatment for social anxiety and related depression. This would not have happened if he had been unable to curtail his unhealthy drinking pattern.

Another example may make it clear how seemingly harmless activities, such as video gaming or working hard, can also become a problem and can then block all progress. Sandy came to see me because her intense and chronic worries frequently upset her and sometimes kept her awake at night. After a few sessions it came to light that she spent every evening and most of the weekend on the internet playing the same video game. When she was playing the game she did not worry or feel so anxious. The problem was that the game took up so much of her time that she had little left for her family or friends. In addition, the game kept her from facing her worries and fears directly. Instead of learning to accept things that were not in her control, she kept herself distracted. Unfortunately, Sandy did not curtail her use of video gaming and I don't believe she was able to make a lot of progress with her excessive worries. Obviously I hope that you will have more success in your recovery, and if you stay with it this is entirely possible.

Healthy Coping Skills

People with anxiety disorders are often not living up to their potential. You may have noticed that you escape, procrastinate or avoid situations that are important to your future. You may be preoccupied by anticipatory anxiety and the thoughts that support it. You may also be preoccupied by unhealthy thoughts in the moment and after the situation. But if you use the ABCS, and do so consistently in the long run, you can free yourself to become much more mindful in the present moment. You can truly listen and communicate more effectively with others. You can learn to experience and enjoy the day. You can increase your freedom and pursue your positive goals in life – if you just commit to staying with it.

Healthy coping skills such as the ABCS are designed to help people face the source of fears and anxiety directly. I do not want people to lock themselves in their bedrooms and practice the ABCS for hours at a time. I want them to use the ABCS, briefly, as they face their feared situation. The many different behaviors, activities and substances that are described in this chapter can serve to distract from and temporarily minimize stress and anxiety in the short run. Some of these behaviors are risky and if pursued for a lengthy period of time can result in addiction and serious health problems. In any case, in the long run these unhealthy escapes block any progress in learning to cope more effectively and also take up so much time and energy that the individual has little left.

Please note: if you think you may have an addiction, I strongly encourage you to seek out a mental health professional who is trained in dealing with both anxiety and addiction. Please see the resources list for help.

Once you have made a personal commitment to do some activity that causes you stress, do it right away, without procrastinating, distracting yourself or escaping. Don't let your fear and anxiety decide that you should back out of the situation. Don't let your fear and anxiety determine when you leave. Begin to incorporate this skill into the ABCS whenever you face a feared situation. It is especially important to use the ABCS when you begin to work on seeking out and facing your fears, either informally or formally (with a written step-by-step plan, as outlined below). By staying with it you can stop and then begin to reverse the negative effects of past fear conditioning. The examples that follow demonstrate how others have used step-by-step plans to face their fears while using this aspect of the ABCS.

Graduated Exposure

Graduated exposure is based on the approach of facing fears in a step-by-step manner. The Subjective Units of Discomfort Scale (SUDS) was developed to help evaluate the amount of stress that each step in a step-by-step plan might cause.[3] All fears and anxieties do not have to be faced at once. However, once the ABCS have been learned it is essential to face feared situations more frequently. That means developing a formal or informal plan to confront these fears, which I would recommend doing with the help of a cognitive behavioral therapist.

It is good to begin with less feared situations and then work up to situations that seem more frightening, until the feared situations have all been faced repeatedly. Frequently, once some of the lower level fears have been successfully faced, the higher level fears do not seem so daunting. Depending on the circumstances, some graduated exposure plans may only take a few days or weeks to complete. However, the general approach needs to be maintained for months or years. It does not all have to be done perfectly, but it is critical to keep going and continue to push the boundaries until freedom from the barriers that fear and anxiety can erect is achieved.

---

3   The technique and scale were first described by Joseph Wolpe in *The Practice of Behavior Therapy* (1969).

In order to develop a formal or an informal graduated exposure plan it is helpful to understand how to rate anxiety and fear. My version of the SUDS follows:

10. Panic

9. Partial panic

8. Very high stress

7. High stress

6. Moderate-high stress

5. Moderate stress

4. Noticeable stress

3. Mild stress – barely noticeable

---

2. Relaxed alertness

1. Very relaxed

As you can see, a score of 1 means "very relaxed" and 2 means "relaxed alertness." It is good to feel relaxed, but alert, when you are solving problems or dealing with a challenging situation. The stress response begins with a score of 3 and goes on up from there. A good way to arrange a plan for facing fears is to estimate how high a SUDS score might be in a particular circumstance. The first step is to pick a goal that represents increased freedom, but that is currently out of reach. The goal may be recommended by a therapist. That goal is broken down into several steps with each step getting predictively somewhat easier (i.e., it has a lower estimated SUDS score). It is important to start with a bottom step that scores no higher than 5. Once the plan is in place, it is necessary to begin to face the situation described in the easiest step, while using coping skills to manage the discomfort. The same step should be faced over and over until it feels more comfortable. A good rule of thumb is to repeat the same step until it has been done confidently two or three times in a row. After some repetition, the actual SUDS score will usually begin to drop. Then it is time to move up to the next step. The process continues on in this way until the highest step in the plan is reached. Of course, the highest step also needs to be faced repeatedly until it can be done confidently several times over. At this point it is time to celebrate the success and think about setting another goal.

Progress may be slowed if the individual beats themselves up for feeling stress in the situation, even if they have faced the feared situation and correctly used their coping skills. Other common problems that block progress include procrastination, avoidance, distraction from the feared aspects of the situation or escaping the situation prematurely; rather than using the S in the ABCS and staying with it. Likewise, and for the many reasons I've outlined in this chapter, when working through a graduated exposure plan, it is not a good idea to take extra anti-anxiety medication, an alcoholic drink or some other calming substance before the exposure. If these substances are taken, the gradual exposure process is likely to take longer.

Because I want you to understand how large fears can be broken down into smaller parts, I have included sample graduated exposure plans for many different types of anxiety covered in this book. The graduated exposure plans that follow were all developed in collaboration between the patient and a cognitive behavioral therapist; as I would recommend, they were all implemented under the supervision of a cognitive behavioral therapist. The general principles behind developing such a plan are as follows:

- Keep it simple and work on one part of the fear at a time.

- Start with the step at the bottom of the list with feared situations that are in the mild to moderate fear level (e.g., up to a SUDS score of 5).

- Fully face the feared situation, without distraction.

- Repeat the same step over and over until it can be done with confidence – then go on to the next, higher step.

- If possible, use the ABCS before, during and after facing the fear-producing situation.

♦ Don't just measure success by levels of anxiety experienced. Measure progress by the commitment to complete the step and the use of anxiety coping skills.

♦ Celebrate successes. Take a well-earned break after successfully completing a step. Have a larger celebration when a graduated exposure plan is successfully completed.

The following samples are designed to give you a good idea about typical graduated exposure plans, but cannot cover each and every situation. While the sample plans show how these plans can be developed, it is not possible to outline the best plan for you. Each graduated exposure plan needs to be tailored to your particular needs. For this reason I recommend that you work with a cognitive behavioral therapist to develop and implement your exact plans.

Social Anxiety

The following two plans demonstrate how to use graduated exposure with social anxiety. When practicing graduated exposure it is wise to use coping skills such as the ABCS. The first example is an initial step-by-step plan for facing fears in one type of social situation.

Sample Graduated Exposure Plan: Social Interaction

Situation	SUDS score
Ask one person if they would like to do something after class	7
Talk to several people after class	5
Talk to one person after class	4
Smile at one person after class	3

The individual who implemented this plan was initially too anxious to interact with her peers at college. She decided to start by smiling at one person after class as this was mildly but not overly stressful: a predicted 3 on the scale. Over time she made lots of progress and was eventually able to complete all the steps on the plan and many more as well. She only moved up the scale after several consecutive successes at the lower levels.

Even though social anxiety often affects people in similar ways, each person is different. Each person needs to have their own plan. Below I have included another sample graduated exposure plan devised for an individual who had already made good progress with social anxiety. This plan was designed to be used in conjunction with a public speaking class or membership in an organization like Toastmasters International, which provides a safe place for individuals to practice better public speaking skills. Public speaking clubs and classes can be found in most cities and towns.

When preparing to give a speech, most people would naturally feel more prepared if they wrote out a word-for-word script of the speech. However, I recommended that he not use a detailed script to give his final speech. The aim was to build his confidence to speak naturally in front of an audience. As such it was better to do the final practice of the speech using only a brief outline. As he practiced giving the speech, he worked down from a word-for-word script to a detailed outline and finally to a brief outline. He was then able to give the speech to the audience without being encumbered by having to memorize or read an exact script. This practice gave him the confidence to be able to make the main points in slightly different ways. Flexibility and good eye contact with the audience then came naturally.

Sample Graduated Exposure Plan: Public Speaking

Situation	SUDS score
Using a brief outline, give a three to five minute speech to a group of 10 to 15 people	9
Using a brief outline, give a three to five minute speech to a friend or family member	7
Using a brief outline, record myself giving a three to five minute speech, alone	6
Using a detailed outline, record myself giving a three to five minute speech, alone	5
Prepare an outline for a three to five minute speech (only do once)	4
Prepare a script for a three to five minute speech (only do once)	3

The individual who used this plan reported that he gave the speech successfully: even though he paused occasionally, he was still able to make his points. He also reported that he used the ABCS just before walking up to the podium. He told me that he made better eye contact with his audience since he was not reading from a detailed script. He went on to complete all ten speeches that were a part of his Toastmasters program. He later reported that this was a very important step in his progress with social anxiety.

If you look at the types of social interactions that often produce anxiety, you will notice that some are much more likely to provoke anxiety than others. For some people, a lot of social interactions will be relatively easy, but "performing" in front of others is very frightening. For some people it is easy to interact with others without much anxiety as long as they are not the center of attention. For many people, public speaking in front of a large group is the most frightening possibility. For others, speaking to a group will not be a problem, as long as there is no potential conflict with anyone and as long as no one shows any disapproval. For some, the larger and more formal the group the more likely it is that they will face lots of anxiety. For many people making a mistake or saying or doing something "silly or foolish" is their worst nightmare. Working with a trained therapist can help to identify and target the specific social anxiety issues that represent a problem for you. A tailored plan can then be developed.

Panic and Agoraphobia

Following are two graduated exposure plans that deal with panic and agoraphobia. The first plan deals with the internal sensations and automatic thoughts that accompany and can cause panic attacks. This plan was developed for an individual who found it extremely distressing whenever she experienced the rapid breathing that is associated with panic attacks. The plan deals with the "fear of the symptoms of fear" aspect of panic disorder. Many people who have panic attacks report that they experience rapid or irregular breathing when they start to get anxious. Many also report a sensation of not getting enough air (even though they are actually getting too much oxygen and not enough carbon dioxide). It is possible to simulate some of the physical sensations of a panic attack by deliberately hyperventilating or by breathing through a straw. By exposing themselves to these physical effects, without the full panic sensation that usually accompanies them, individuals can learn to reduce their fear of panic attacks. With some individuals straw breathing is more effective at producing a realistic simulation and for others rapid breathing is sufficient. This individual began by breathing rapidly for 30 seconds and then, when she became comfortable with that level, she built up to two minutes in graduated steps. We then added muscle tension and finally the automatic thoughts that usually accompanied her panic. After she had successfully completed all these steps during our sessions in my office, I asked her to do this at home once a day, in between her therapy sessions.

Sample Graduated Exposure Plan: Fear of Panic Attack

Please note: this plan should be supervised by a cognitive behavioral therapist. In addition, check with your doctor before starting work on the plan if you have any medical problems.

Situation	SUDS score
Breathing rapidly, tensing muscles and thinking automatic thoughts for two minutes	10
Breathing rapidly while tensing muscles in body for two minutes	9
Breathing rapidly for two minutes	8
Breathing rapidly for one and a half minutes	7
Breathing rapidly for one minute	6
Breathing rapidly for 30 seconds	5

It took six or seven sessions before she was able to complete this plan in my office. Each time she completed an exposure she was encouraged to use the ABCS to help her recover from any stress. Thereafter, she was able to practice once a day, at home, with the step that previously she had predicted as a 10. She later told me that by voluntarily facing this fear she found that her fear of panic was much reduced. Her actual level of SUDS when practicing at home was much lower than originally predicted: never more than a minimal level. She reported no additional full panic attacks after six months of follow-up.

The next plan focuses on the most common type of agoraphobia in which the individual avoids going beyond their "safe zone," without the presence of a trusted helper because they fear another panic attack is likely. For most people their agoraphobia is worse when they believe that the situation is very similar to a previous one in which they did have a panic attack. For many individuals the situation is also worse if no one is there to help (e.g., if only strangers are present or no one else is around). Another common factor which can produce more stress and dread is when the individual feels "trapped" and as if they can't escape out into the fresh air. When people have a panic attack the almost universal reaction is to want to escape the situation and get out into the open air where they can breathe deeply. It is almost as if they are being attacked and strangled by a wild beast. Of course there is no such thing actually happening. It is really a false alarm, but it can trigger a huge physiological and emotional response (the fight or flight response described in the introduction).

This plan was developed for an individual who had not been able to get back behind the wheel after experiencing a panic attack while driving at speed on a busy expressway. As always, she started with the bottom step (the lowest estimated SUDS score) and repeatedly did that step until more confidence was acquired and the actual SUDS level dropped significantly. After several consecutive successes at the first step she then moved up to the next higher step.

Please note: this plan should be implemented under the supervision of a cognitive behavioral therapist. Do not attempt this plan yourself if you have had recent tickets or accidents involving driving, or if your medical doctor has told you not to drive.

Sample Graduated Exposure Plan: Fear of Leaving the "Safe Zone"

Situation	SUDS score
Driving (alone) 10 miles on the expressway (or past seven exits) then exiting	10
Driving (alone) 5 miles on the expressway (or past four exits) then exiting	9
Driving (alone) 2 miles on the expressway (or past one exit), then exiting	8
Driving (with trusted helper) 10 miles on the expressway (or past seven exits) then exiting	7
Driving (with trusted helper) 5 miles on the expressway (or past four exits) then exiting	6
Driving (with trusted helper) 2 miles on the expressway (or past one exit) then exiting	5

After seven or eight weeks she reported that she was now on the highest step of the plan. Soon thereafter, she completed the plan and reported that she had much more confidence when driving, both on and off the expressway. She was then able to travel much more independently.

GAD

This sample graduated exposure plan deals with worries. It was developed to deal with the compulsive worries of a father with an adult daughter. He often worried and obsessed when his daughter traveled. The obsessions took the form of jumping to conclusions about all the possible catastrophes that might occur, such as her being raped or killed by a stranger, or being killed in a crash. To gain reassurance he called her dozens of times each day, but this level of checking was inappropriate and put their relationship under strain. The sample plan that follows targets these excessive phone calls. The father was encouraged to use the ABCS to cope with the stress of not calling. He was also encouraged to discuss the plan with his daughter.

Sample Graduated Exposure Plan: Worry about Family Catastrophes

Situation	SUDS score
Call daughter, who's traveling, no more than once every other day	10
Call daughter, who's traveling, no more than once a day	9
Call daughter, who's traveling, no more than twice a day	7
Call daughter, who's traveling, no more than five times a day	5
Call daughter, who's traveling, no more than ten times a day	4

The father had difficulty starting on this plan, but after he had talked to his daughter and committed to work on the plan his progress improved and after several months he had reached the highest step. He told me his daughter was independent and appreciated his success in limiting his calls to a more reasonable number. At the last follow-up session he reported that using the ABCS had helped as he faced his fears.

Specific Phobia

As we will see in Chapter 7, there are many different specific phobias and it would not be possible to address each object of fear here. This plan for beginning to work on a severe phobia of dogs represents how graduated exposure can be put to work with any type of phobia. To implement this plan, the individual asked a friend to borrow their small puppy, which sleeps in a puppy cage. The friend placed the cage, with the puppy inside it, at the far end of a ten foot long room. Using the ABCS to help him, the individual then gradually moved closer and closer to the puppy. As you can see from the plan that follows, several more incremental plans would have to be completed in order to completely deal with his severe phobia.

Sample Graduated Exposure Plan: Phobia of Dogs

Situation	SUDS score
Take one more step and kneel by the cage and stay until I feel confident	10
Take two more steps toward the puppy and stay until I feel confident	9
Take two more steps toward the puppy and stay until I feel confident	8
Take two more steps toward the puppy and stay until I feel confident	7
Take two more steps toward the puppy and stay until I feel confident	6
Take one step toward the puppy and stay until I feel confident	5

By gradually increasing proximity to the object of the phobia, in a controlled way, his fear gradually diminished. He was able to reach the highest step of the plan after several lengthy home sessions with the puppy. It was then easier for him to cope when he unexpectedly faced a puppy or dog while going about his day. Of course, more work was needed before he became comfortable with dogs that were not in cages.

Exercise

Feared situations may be external to the individual (e.g., fear of a particular object or experience) or internal (e.g., produced by worry thoughts or frightening memories). Pick a feared situation that is not physically dangerous, but is related to your core fear. Make sure that the feared situation is not overwhelming. Pick something that is just outside your comfort zone. Now, make a commitment to voluntarily face this feared situation and stay with it for a period of time necessary to employ each part of the ABCS. When you are in the situation, be sure to not use unhealthy escape behavior to try to escape the fear. Instead follow through and use your coping skills. This kind of practice can help you improve your ability to stay with it.

Chapter 5

Coping with Related Depression

"Stop aspiring to be anyone other than your own best self: for that does fall within your control."

Epictetus, *The Art of Living*

Many people who suffer with anxiety disorders also experience depression. If you take the big picture view, depression may cause anxiety, anxiety may cause depression or some other factors may contribute to both. In my own clinical experience, I have seen many cases where untreated anxiety disorders cause more and more frustration by increasing the limitations on the individual and causing them to miss opportunities. People who lose jobs, are unable to apply for suitable jobs, drop out of college, avoid relationships or end relationships prematurely, or whose lives are otherwise controlled by anxiety grieve such losses and can be more prone to depression. Many of these people can identify a time when they had problems with anxiety, but little to no depression. After depression starts it may be episodic, in which case it typically follows a new setback, or it may be chronic and continue for years. For many of these people, I believe that in a very real sense the accumulation of losses caused by the anxiety disorder resulted in their depressed mood. Of course, if your depression predates your anxiety disorder, is very severe or is your primary health concern you should focus on its treatment, which is beyond the focus of this book. This chapter addresses depression that is not completely debilitating and is related to, or the result of, a persistent anxiety disorder.

Please note: if your depression is severe or if you are having thoughts about harming yourself you need to immediately seek an evaluation from a mental health professional.

The purpose of this chapter is to assist you in dealing with the type of depression that seems to be linked to untreated anxiety disorders. If you suffer from anxiety and related depression it is important to face both issues. It takes lots of effort to recover from an anxiety disorder and a depressed mood undermines the motivation that is required for recovery. I believe it is important to address any depression someone may be experiencing early in their treatment for anxiety. When I work with a patient who has depression along with anxiety, I often begin by helping them to develop more realistic goals. These kinds of healthy, realistic goals are based on the ideas around acceptance, which are outlined under the A of the ABCS.

Setting Realistic Personal Goals

As a psychologist, I had the opportunity to work with a fairly large number of very successful salespeople. Some had been at or near the top of their field, having won regional or even national sales awards. They often seemed to face a similar problem, which ran along these lines: "I was doing extremely well at my job until one month my sales revenues dipped. My boss asked about it and I became increasingly concerned. I started to dread making calls to try to set up appointments. When the figures came out for the next month my numbers had dropped even more. I lost all my motivation and started to have trouble getting out of bed in the morning. This happened six months ago. I still feel so down. What is wrong with me?"

This situation seems to be a classic case of misplaced responsibility. What these salespeople usually had in common was that they took responsibility for things that were not in their direct control and didn't take responsibility for those things that were. Inevitably, when the full story came out, it became clear that the first month's decline in sales was the result of factors beyond their control, for example, a worsening economy in the product sector, a news story that affected their key product or a personal illness that interfered with work performance. However, after the first month's dip in sales, the individual became apprehensive about their ability to sell and began to dread making phone calls to set up appointments. With fewer calls there were fewer appointments, and with fewer appointments sales dropped even more. Concerned and agitated, the individual started to have trouble getting out of bed and their depression became worse and worse.

A salesperson's gross figures are not completely in their control: there will always be other factors influencing the market. What is in their control is to get up on time, get dressed and go to work. Then, when at work, they make telephone calls to set up appointments and follow through on those appointments. So, rather than setting a personal goal of a certain sales total per month, a more realistic personal goal would be to make "x" number of telephone calls per day. When you take care of the things that are in your control then that will often have a very large positive influence on the important things that are not in your direct control.

When you set personal goals, make sure that they are all realistic goals (i.e., things that are in your control). See the examples of corrected goals that follow. Remember, even corrected goals cannot be guaranteed since unforeseen circumstances may sometimes occur.

Examples of Corrected Goals

"I cannot feel anxious anymore," can be corrected to: "I will learn and apply anxiety coping skills to face my fears."

"I must not feel depressed anymore," can be corrected to: "I will learn and apply depression coping skills to stop avoiding what I need to face."

"I must get married to someone who will love me forever," can be corrected to: "I want to get out and meet people, then be open to deepening the relationship, acting in a trustworthy manner, etc."

"I must have a job making 'x' per year," can be corrected to: "I will finish my résumé then upload it to reputable web sites. I will call all of my friends and acquaintances and ask if they know of any leads, I will follow up on all leads and apply for whatever reasonable jobs that I can find."

"I cannot allow my child (or my spouse or my best friend) to make such a huge mistake," can be corrected to: "I will speak to them and try to be a positive influence, but I need to accept that I can't prevent the mistake, if they are intent on doing what they want anyway. No one has that much power over others."

"I will graduate college in two years with all 'A's," can be corrected to: "I will sign up for a full load of classes every semester, commit to studying for all tests and complete all homework assignments."

"I will be the greatest parent," can be corrected to: "I will reduce or eliminate any sarcastic comments and give positive feedback on a regular basis. I will demonstrate a healthy lifestyle to my child."

As you can see from the story about the top salespeople, it is extremely important to set realistic goals. These corrected goals can provide you with a model for ensuring that your own goals are realistic. Setting unrealistic goals for yourself can have devastating consequences and can produce anxiety, frustration and depression. It doesn't even matter if these goals are not formally written down. The assumptions that we carry around in our heads are probably more important than any written goals: these implicit unrealistic assumptions can harm you just as much. Unrealistic goals based on assumptions are almost always impossible to attain, but realistic goals can be worked on successfully, which brings hope, not hopelessness.

"Comparisonitus"

The tendency to frequently compare ourselves to others can be another contributor to depression. I call this negative process "comparisonitus." We do not benefit from constant comparisons where we devalue ourselves while looking at everyone else through rose-colored glasses. At the age of 18, we do not all line up on the "starting line of adult life" with the same strengths and weaknesses. Some people have fortunate genetic endowments, some have had wonderful childhood and adolescent experiences, some have not experienced serious physical or emotional trauma and some have not had stressful day-to-day lives. All of these benefits have come to them largely by external chance, not because they "earned it." On the other hand, some people, through no choice of their own, have experienced just the opposite. When we meet someone we cannot know about their past or any of these factors. Even when we get to know them, we shouldn't make these comparisons. We would be much better off if we compared ourselves using our own measures of success: how are we doing now compared to last year or last month? How does this compare with our realistic goals? We need to stop beating ourselves up and focus on developing our own best self.

Taking Charge of What You Can Control

No one can just "snap out of it" and make depression go away. However, we can all learn and use coping skills and that can have a positive influence on how we feel. The next section details how to begin this process. Before reading the Ten Rules for Coping with Depression, think about what your most important personal goals are. You may include goals about your work, your emotional difficulties, your relationships, your values and your job or school. Please make sure your goals are *realistic* and represent things that are really under your *complete control*. It is important to think about your goals because part of the Ten Rules involves working on them.

Getting active when you are depressed is very difficult, but it offers a step-by-step path toward doing and feeling better. Productive activities will benefit you in the long run and these activities need to include some actions that support your personal goals. Even though you may feel like doing little else, laying on your bed or couch and obsessing and ruminating will only make the depression worse. Once you have a clear understanding of the things you can and cannot control you can direct your energy where it will do some good and let go of the rest. The Ten Rules represent things that you can learn to bring under your control that will have a positive influence on how you feel. You may make copies of the Ten Rules so you will be able to complete the checklist every day for several weeks. If you work at it over time, the Ten Rules can eventually become part of your healthy habits.[1]

---

1 The Ten Rules are based on my clinical experience with thousands of patients over the years, combined with attending countless conferences and also reading and reviewing hundreds of books and articles that deal with these topics. It is difficult to identify all of the sources that may have influenced the development of the Ten Rules. However, I should note that research done by those who developed Activity Scheduling (Beck et al., 1979), the later work regarding Behavioral Activation (Kanter, Busch and Rusch, 2009) and also the work on Positive Psychology (Seligman, 2006) all had an influence on my development of the Ten Rules.

The Ten Rules for
Coping with Depression

In order to benefit the most from using these coping skills it is important to first write down your personal goals and then spend some time each day engaged in productive activities that support your goals.

My most important personal goals are:

_____

_____

_____

_____

_____

_____

Review all ten items at the end of each day, placing a tick next to each day of the week when each of the items is completed.

1. Get active: get out of bed, do morning hygiene and get dressed.

    Mon: __ Tue: __ Wed: __ Thurs: __ Fri: __ Sat: __ Sun: __

2. Do something productive that helps you toward one of your personal goals, or is a necessary activity or task, then take a rest/recreation break. Repeat this pattern of work then rest (or play) again and again throughout the day.

    Mon: __ Tue: __ Wed: __ Thurs: __ Fri: __ Sat: __ Sun: __

3. Do mild exercise: walk for 20–30 minutes, ride bike, swim, etc.

    Mon: __ Tue: __ Wed: __ Thurs: __ Fri: __ Sat: __ Sun: __

From *The ABCS of Coping with Anxiety* © James D. Cowart, PhD 2017

4. Practice countering unhealthy, unrealistic thoughts.

   Mon: __ Tue: __ Wed: __ Thurs: __ Fri: __ Sat: __ Sun: __

5. Talk to friends or family, provided that they are emotionally supportive.

   Mon: __ Tue: __ Wed: __ Thurs: __ Fri: __ Sat: __ Sun: __

6. If a friend or family member is not supportive, take care of yourself by setting limits and acting assertively. Alternatively, avoid spending too much time with them.

   Mon: __ Tue: __ Wed: __ Thurs: __ Fri: __ Sat: __ Sun: __

7. Identify things you used to enjoy and pursue one such activity several times each week.

   Mon: __ Tue: __ Wed: __ Thurs: __ Fri: __ Sat: __ Sun: __

8. Write down one good thing that happened along with the cause(s).

   Mon: __ Tue: __ Wed: __ Thurs: __ Fri: __ Sat: __ Sun: __

9. Take care of yourself. If you are taking an anti-depressant, take it consistently as prescribed. Attend any therapy appointments you may have.

   Mon: __ Tue: __ Wed: __ Thurs: __ Fri: __ Sat: __ Sun: __

10. If you are trying to control something that is impossible to control, practice accepting that reality and letting go – or at least begin to act as if you are accepting it.

    Mon: __ Tue: __ Wed: __ Thurs: __ Fri: __ Sat: __ Sun: __

Rules 5 and 6 deal exclusively with relationships, as our interactions with others can have a significant effect on how we feel. It is especially important to begin to set limits and act more assertively when faced with unhealthy or "toxic" relationships. Setting limits can mean talking to someone less frequently or for less time. This can be accomplished by speaking up directly or by making an excuse. For example, "Please call before you drop over because I may have to run an errand at that time" or "I can only talk for five minutes now, because I am very busy." Speaking assertively is important in all relationships, not just unhealthy ones. It means expressing yourself directly and in a clear voice, but without sarcasm or anger. It means addressing the specific issue; not judging or attacking the other person's character (e.g., "Please call if you are going to be late" rather than "I guess you are not courteous enough to call."). Spending more time with people who are supportive will have a positive influence on your depression. Rule 10 is about acceptance of all things not in your control. For example, if you are trying to control someone else, to rescue them from their problems, then you will need to accept the limits of your power. If you are trying to directly control your own emotions then you will need to accept that this is not possible: no one totally controls their inner emotions. Like all of us, you need to fully accept your human nature.

The purpose of the Ten Rules is to help you see that there are important things that are under your control, and that your actions can have a positive influence on your depressed mood on a daily basis. If you have depression then use the checklist on a daily basis for several weeks so you can begin to see what you are doing regularly and what may be missing. With persistence you can begin to have ticks under all ten rules most days. Eventually, these healthy activities can become habits that don't require as much thought and effort.

Exercise

Complete the Ten Rules checklist each day. Remember, Rule 2 deals with productive activities including the ones you've identified as your personal goals. Also remember that no one is perfect so there will be ups and downs in your practice of the Ten Rules. However, if you maintain a realistic view of the change process (i.e., it is perfectly human to take three steps forward and two steps back) you can keep moving forward. Continue to use the checklist until the rules become your own learned habits. When you have made some gains with your depression you will be better able to do the work necessary to recover from your anxiety disorder.

Chapter 6

COPING WITH RELATED ANGER AND IMPULSIVITY

"Anyone can become angry … That is easy. But to be angry with the right person, to the right degree, at the right time, for the right purpose, and in the right way – that is not easy."

ARISTOTLE, *NICOMACHEAN ETHICS*

One of the ways in which human beings react to anxiety and stress is by becoming angry and irritable. Anger is a part of our fight or flight response: our readiness for confrontation can be triggered by stress. When we get stressed we sometimes react with anger, but unfortunately, we often can become angry with people who had nothing to do with why we were stressed to begin with. In addition we can overreact to small or trivial issues when we feel lots of stress. Sometimes when we are trying to cope with an anxiety disorder our own anger and irritability can grow and increase to a point that can threaten relationships. On the other hand, sometimes others can behave in ways that are genuinely harmful to us and we need to be able to speak up. If the behavior of others is repeatedly causing us harm or stress, and this is not due to our own unhealthy thinking or our angry outbursts, it is important to be able to speak up directly and clearly, without sarcasm or verbal aggression. We need to remember that anger is a normal human emotion, but it must be expressed appropriately and to the correct person. This type of communication is called assertiveness. The purpose of this chapter is to help you stop judgmental, aggressive or sarcastic comments, that may also be misdirected, and to instead rely on assertive communication when it is needed.

Stopping Impulsive and Excessive Anger Outbursts

You are no doubt familiar with the expression "Don't kick the dog (or cat)." This refers to the tendency to lash out at someone, or some pet, when we are really upset with someone or something else. Our emotions can get the better of us and we can react impulsively and aggressively to something that had nothing to do with the original problem or conflict. It is also very easy to over-react to a seemingly small or trivial problem with a huge expression of anger. Perhaps a person who hasn't spoken up about a problem that has gone on for years begins to feel so overwhelmed by the many other sources of stress that they explode at the other person with much more anger than is necessary. These kinds of outbursts can be very harmful to long-term relationships. People who are the frequent target of these types of over-the-top outbursts can grow resentful and fearful and are likely to begin to avoid the person who engages in this behavior. Or they may react with similar over-the-top outbursts of their own. These kinds of reactions are a part of our human nature and are hard to avoid.

However, there are coping skills that can be used to reduce and eliminate excessive angry outbursts.

I developed the STOP technique to help people who realized that their anger was excessive and frequently felt remorse for their outbursts. The STOP technique can also be used as a tool to help reduce or eliminate other impulsive and self-defeating behaviors such as smoking, alcohol and drug abuse, excessive shopping and eating and so on. The STOP technique has some similarities to the ABCS. It is important to remember that the STOP technique is about self-control. It is not about other people saying "stop" to you. That kind of external control would likely produce more anger and would consequently be a negative influence on the relationship. The STOP technique involves an individual choosing to reduce their own impulsive behavior by taking the time to de-stress and think realistically before speaking or acting.

The STOP Technique

S SAY "STOP" TO YOURSELF. When you have an urge to scream, swear, or engage in sarcastic comments or other impulsive behavior, just say (or think) the word "stop."

T TAKE SOME SLOW BREATHS. Each time you breathe out let go of extra tension throughout your whole body. Unclench your fists and relax the muscles in your neck and back. Let go of the tension as you let go of the breath.

O ORGANIZE YOUR THOUGHTS. Consider all the long-term costs of whatever it is you have an urge to do. Compare those long-term costs to the possible short-term gains that you may want at this moment. Is it really worth it? Are your thoughts about this situation healthy and realistic? Are your thoughts based on evidence and logic?

P PROCEED WITH YOUR CHOICE. Now that you have used your coping skills your choice will probably be a better one.

Tom's Story

Here is an example from my clinical experience to illustrate how to use the STOP technique with anger. (Again, names and some facts have been changed to protect confidentiality.)

Tom suffered from high levels of social anxiety combined with episodes of depression. Sometimes at work he felt overwhelmed by his overly controlling boss. Sometimes his frustrations boiled over at home and he lashed out verbally at his wife and teenage daughter over what he later admitted were "minor problems." One day after dealing with his boss at work Tom arrived home and found his daughter talking on the phone while playing her favorite music at a very loud volume. Tom had the urge to scream at her and say sarcastic things, but instead he took the time to use the STOP technique. He thought the word "stop" then took some slow steady breaths while letting go of the tension that had been accumulating all day. Then he thought about how he wanted to have a better relationship with his daughter who was soon to be away at college. He realized that their relationship was far more important than the temporary feeling of righteous indignation he might feel if he blew up at her. Tom decided to use a calm voice to ask her to turn down the volume on her music.

Tom also learned to use the STOP technique to interrupt his tendency to ruminate about all the perceived negative things others had done to him. On the way home from work he would often mentally replay times when his wife or daughter had done something to upset him. When he arrived home he was already tense and angry and any little thing could set him off. Eventually, Tom learned that he could use the STOP technique to turn off these repetitive negative images that seemed to pop into his mind. He learned that, while he could not always keep these thoughts and images from popping into his mind, he didn't have to "push the play button" and rewatch them for minutes at a time. He learned to stop these thoughts and images and to direct his attention onto something else.

Please note: if you are at risk of physically hurting others you need to immediately seek an evaluation from a mental health professional.

Developing Assertiveness Skills

Assertiveness means dealing with conflict in a direct and clear manner, without verbal aggression (swearing, screaming, sarcastic comments or negative judgments about the other person). Assertiveness means dealing with the specific facts and the particular behavior that is a problem for you, not engaging in interpretations or judgments. On a continuum of how individuals can deal with conflict, assertiveness is in the middle, between passivity on one end and aggressiveness on the other. It is the moderate, balanced approach that allows you to get your point across without being rude. It reduces the chance that the other person will take offence. When conflict occurs, if you almost always respond in a passive manner and don't speak up, you will likely feel more and more stressed and overwhelmed and you may even resort to sabotage (consciously or unconsciously) of the other's wants and needs. For example, if one person in a relationship usually acts passively and the other usually acts aggressively, the more passive individual may become so quietly resentful and angry that they deliberately "forget" something the other wants. Alternatively, in contrast to your usual passivity you may overreact and have an emotional blow-up. If you are never able to act assertively in your most important relationships it is easy to begin to feel depressed and to think that your life is out of control. Good relationships depend upon each person being able to speak assertively, at least some of the time. It is one of the ways that people can learn to really know each other's thoughts, feelings and desires.

At the simplest level there are at least two basic components to an assertive communication: (1) stating the specific behavior (or lack of it) that was a problem to you and (2) stating the effect it had on you (e.g., extra work, wasted effort and/or the negative way you felt about it). If you want to ask the person to make a change, the assertive communication needs to include a third point: stating what you would like the other person to do differently in the future. When you deliver an assertive communication, do so with good eye contact, speaking in a clear voice, without signs of excessive anger such as finger pointing or clenched fists. Finally, the assertive communication should be brief, not a part of a lengthy, angry lecture.

Assertive Statements

The following examples show how assertiveness can be used in everyday life.

> *"When you left your toys lying in the driveway, I had to park the car on the street then move the toys before I could pull into the driveway. It was annoying for me."* If you want your child to handle this differently in the future you could add, *"In the future, when you play with your toys in the driveway, please put them away before I come home."*

> *"If you don't call when you are going to be late for dinner, the food gets dried out and I get frustrated. Please call me if you are going to be more than 20 minutes late."*

Aggressive Statements

The next two examples contrast this assertive approach with the aggressive or sarcastic handling of the same two situations.

> *"You never pick up your toys! You have no consideration for others. You will probably end up living as a hermit."*

"You can't do the simplest thing for me! How many times have I asked you to call if you won't be home for dinner? You don't care about me."

I am sure that you can see the vast difference between verbal aggression and assertiveness. You may also notice that the second set of examples contain unrealistic thinking. If a partner forgets to call, it could be because they've had a really busy day and haven't had the opportunity. It doesn't mean that they don't care. By focusing on the action and its consequences, we can ensure we are using evidence and logic and avoid jumping to conclusions.

When you first start to use assertiveness it may seem awkward, but if you continue to practice being assertive it can become very natural. Assertiveness does not guarantee that you will get a good response from the other person, but it does make it more likely. Assertiveness takes the courage to speak up combined with the patience to control how you express your anger. Remember if you never speak up this passivity may hurt you in the long run and if you frequently blow up it will probably hurt your relationships. Assertiveness is the healthy pathway between these two extremes. As with any tool you have to decide when to use it. There are times, for example if you are being physically threatened, when assertiveness may not be the most appropriate response. It is a good idea to pick the time and place when you will act assertively. You don't need to be assertive 100% of the time. However, if you almost never react with assertiveness you will likely experience some of the negative consequences described here.

Exercise

If you are experiencing episodes of anger, practice using the STOP technique to help you reduce or eliminate angry outbursts or other impulsive behavior.

If you have difficulty speaking up for yourself, practice using assertiveness skills when you want to make clear to someone the effect their behavior has had on you. You don't need to use it in every situation, but if the same problem situation keeps happening over and over, then you probably need to speak up. Your loved ones may also need to speak up about the effect your behavior or actions have had on them, so practice listening and communicating openly together.

Chapter 7

Using the ABCS with Different Types of Anxiety

> "I suppose it is tempting, if the only tool you have is a hammer, to treat everything as if it were a nail."
>
> ABRAHAM MASLOW, *The Psychology of Science*

Many individuals experience what are known as classic anxiety disorders, which include panic disorder, agoraphobia, social anxiety, GAD, OCD, illness anxiety and PTSD, as well as specific phobias.[1] Many other individuals experience excessive levels of stress and anxiety, triggered by negative life changes that are difficult to adjust to. Individuals may experience moments of high anxiety or even panic as well as periods of time that are filled with lower levels of anxiety or dread as a result of these issues. Typically, individuals will engage in behaviors involving avoidance of and escape from situations that trigger the fear or anxiety. Each problem and disorder is distinct and organized around a characteristic, core set of fears. It is not helpful to try to avoid your core fear or to rely exclusively on distraction techniques. Instead it is important to identify the core fear(s) you have and then tailor the coping skills around this specific issue. In this chapter, the ABCS are adapted to focus on their application for a particular core fear. Recovery comes from using your coping skills to repeatedly face

---

1   As mentioned earlier, if your condition has not been formally diagnosed, you can find useful screening tools on the ADAA web site (http://www.adaa.org/). The screening tools are located in the "Live and Thrive" section and will help you to determine which conditions may represent a problem for you. There is also a screening tool for depression. However, you should still seek help from a qualified professional. Please do not rely solely on self-diagnosis.

the core fear until it is weakened. Frequently, the core fear can be broken down using a step-by-step plan, as shown in Chapter 4.

You learned in Chapters 1 to 4 about the general characteristics of each of the coping skills that comprise the ABCS. This chapter will briefly review these basic ABCS and then describe the core fear for each of the anxiety disorders listed above, as well as examples of core fear(s) that may be associated with negative life changes. Each of these examples includes a set of tailored ABCS for coping with that particular core fear. Each set of ABCS is like a set of tools matched to that particular core fear. Read through the following sections to identify your own core fear(s) and then use the relevant ABCS in your recovery. If you have more than one type of anxiety then use the set of coping skills for the particular core fear that you are facing at the moment. In addition, some people may have related depression to contend with, and other people may be experiencing anger or substance abuse. Everyone is different and has different needs. This chapter will demonstrate how the ABCS can be tailored to fit your individual needs. *At the end of the chapter you will find an exercise to help you construct your own personalized version for future use.*

The stories from my clinical experience that appear throughout this chapter illustrate how the ABCS can yield great results, when they are tailored to the individual and their core fear(s). Of course, in the field of mental health treatment there is nothing more important than a patient's confidentiality. As such, identifying information has been changed to protect the confidentiality of former patients. Some of the stories are based on composites of two or more cases, but they are true in the sense that they accurately portray the course of successful treatment. I hope you can see from these stories that real change is possible, but not easy.

The Basic ABCS

A is for acceptance of all things you cannot control. Our human nature doesn't allow us to control our emotions and the automatic thoughts (or memories) that sometimes pop into our minds. Our human nature also does not allow us to control what others think or do, or protect ourselves, or our loved ones, from all harm. We must accept the uncertainty and risk that is part of life. We may have some influence over some aspects, but we do not have complete control. So, in particular, don't get mad at yourself for feeling anxious or having other bad feelings. Acceptance means letting go of things you cannot control so you can focus on things you can do something about, like what you do and say, and what choices you make in the present moment. So once you have done your best to provide a positive influence in a given situation, you need to learn to let it go. If you have a good understanding of human nature you also know that choosing to voluntarily face unrealistic fears is the best way to reduce them (just as getting active, productive and reaching out to those who care about you are some of the best ways to improve your mood).

B is for breathing slowly and naturally while you relax your muscle tension. High levels of anxiety or panic often trigger rapid, shallow breathing (i.e., hyperventilation). Rapid, shallow breathing increases stress by reducing the amount of carbon dioxide in your blood so much that you feel lightheaded. So, when you get anxious, choose to breathe in a slow and natural manner, drawing the breath right down into your diaphragm, and make sure you breathe out for as long as you breathe in. This will provide a positive influence on how you are feeling.

C is for countering any unrealistic or catastrophic thoughts with the truth. "I can't stand feeling like this!" can be countered with: "I am learning to cope with these feelings." "I shouldn't feel anxious!" can be countered with: "I need to accept that my emotions are not under my direct control." "I shouldn't have a thought like this!" can be countered with: "This is an automatic thought and thoughts are not the same as actions." "Other people will judge me and think I am an idiot!" can be countered with: "I cannot control or even know what others think of me so I need to do what I think is right and then let it go." "I can't stand it when this memory pops into my mind!" can be countered with: "I can't block out all memories, but a memory is not the same as being there." Countering unrealistic thoughts with thoughts based on evidence and logic can have a positive influence on how you feel.

S is for staying with it so you can fully face your unrealistic fears and anxieties until they are reduced. It means not escaping or avoiding the situation or getting temporary relief, for example by using alcohol or drugs, or repeatedly checking for reassurance. It means fully being there as you voluntarily choose to face the fear. However, you don't have to face all your fears at once. You can take them on in a step-by-step manner. But once you have picked a feared situation to face, stay with it until you have finished your commitment.

Adaptation of the Basic ABCS to Different Core Fears

In each of the examples that follow, you will find specific adaptations that relate to the different core fears. When you use the ABCS, you will find it more helpful to add the specific points that relate to how you are feeling and the issues you need to focus on. However, remember that all the information from the basic ABCS still applies, combined with the new additions for the particular core fear(s).

Panic Disorder with Agoraphobia

Panic disorder is sometimes called "fear of fear." Its main feature is that the individual experiences situations where lower levels of stress and anxiety can quickly come to trigger panic level fear. Some of the symptoms can make things worse very quickly (e.g., hyperventilation can cause lightheadedness, excessive muscle tension can cause trembling and, of course, unrealistic thinking can trigger additional symptoms of all kinds). Sometimes these panic attacks can occur with little or no warning. Circumstances in which the individual has had a previous panic attack become difficult to face without high levels of stress. Avoidance can in some cases lead to what is known as agoraphobia (fear and avoidance of going out alone into public spaces).

The core fear in panic disorder is that in the midst of an attack the individual will lose control, be institutionalized or have a heart attack and die. A related belief is that it is impossible to tolerate these feelings of anxiety and panic, especially when there is not a friend or family member nearby to help. Recovery comes from choosing to repeatedly face your fears, as you use your coping skills. Use the tailored version of the ABCS that follows to better cope with panic and agoraphobia.

The ABCS for Coping with Panic Disorder with Agoraphobia

A is for acceptance. We don't control our own emotions and the automatic thoughts that sometimes pop into our minds. In particular, don't get mad at yourself for feeling anxious or having other symptoms such as sweating, shaking, feeling flushed, heart pounding or skipping a beat or feeling disoriented, etc. Accept that scary thoughts may pop into your mind, like "I'm going to die or lose control," or "I am trapped and can't escape." Accept that facing your fears is the best way to reduce them and accept that you have control over your behavior and choices even when you are experiencing panic. Acceptance can have a very positive influence on your anxiety and panic.

B is for breathing slowly and naturally while you relax your muscle tension. When panicky feelings occur they often trigger rapid, shallow breathing (i.e., hyperventilation). Rapid, shallow breathing increases stress by reducing the amount of carbon dioxide in your blood so much that you feel lightheaded. So, when you get anxious, choose to breathe in a slow and natural manner and make sure you breathe out as much as you breathe in. As you breathe out, let go of muscle tension throughout your whole body. You can take charge of your breathing and your muscle tension, and if you do, you will provide a positive influence on how you are feeling and on your symptoms of panic and anxiety.

C is for countering any unrealistic or catastrophic thoughts with the truth. For example, "I can't stand feeling like this!" can be countered with: "I am learning to cope with these feelings." "I shouldn't feel anxious!" can be countered with: "I need to accept that my emotions are not under my direct control." "I am dying of a heart attack!" can be countered with: "My doctor has evaluated my health and says that I am not dying." "I'm losing control!" can be countered with: "This is just a feeling, not the reality." "When I feel anxious, I need to go home!" can be countered with: "I need to stay with it, by using the ABCS to cope, and finish the task that I set for myself." Countering unrealistic thoughts with thoughts based on evidence and logic can have a positive influence on panic and anxiety.

S is for staying with it so you can fully face your unrealistic fears and anxieties until they are reduced. If you are in a store or another building when you start feeling panicky, try to stay where you are while you use the ABCS. If need be go to the bathroom or to your car, use the ABCS, then stay with it by returning to the situation. If you are traveling use the ABCS where you are then continue traveling. If need be, take a brief break to use the ABCS then continue your journey. Over time, staying with it can help you build confidence in facing what you need to face, so your panic and agoraphobia can be reduced.

Kirsten's Story

Kirsten is a college graduate with a good mind, but she tearfully told me in our first therapy session that she had not been able to find a job since graduating over a year ago. Due to her anxiety, college had been difficult for her, but she had persevered.

However, now things were getting much worse. She had experienced multiple panic attacks, several of which occurred when she was driving. She worried about having another of these attacks and this added to her fear of going out. She got very anxious in job interviews and in recent months she had given up on even trying to find a job. She had a boyfriend and saw him frequently, but otherwise didn't go out much. She was afraid of being judged by others. In many different social situations she got very anxious, which made her feel nauseated. Then she worried that she would throw up in front of others and that would be her worst nightmare. Over time she began to avoid more and more social situations – especially if they involved unstructured conversation and eating. Finally, she reported that in the months before her first session, she had experienced more intense and frequent feelings of being overwhelmed and feeling hopeless about the future.[2]

A psychiatrist had previously prescribed an anti-depressant to help with her depression and anxiety. However, after a few months it became clear that these issues remained. We continued our weekly sessions and she first focused on setting realistic personal goals and then worked on the Ten Rules for Coping with Depression (as outlined in Chapter 5). After some success with using these rules, she also began to use tailored ABCS to cope with her panic attacks, agoraphobia and social anxiety. She learned the importance of being assertive when negotiating the social activities she agreed to take part in with her boyfriend and she also made a commitment to stay in the social situation for a specified length of time. After several exposures she became increasingly confident that if she accepted her own anxiety she could cope with it for the agreed time period. Although she had several more partial panic attacks she never threw up and she began to realize that this was not actually very likely, unless she was physically ill. Below you will find Kirsten's additions to the ABCS for coping with social anxiety,

---

2   Interviews and clinical questionnaires, such as the Social Phobia Inventory (SPIN), the Mobility Inventory for Agoraphobia (MI) and the Beck Depression Inventory (BDI), had identified several primary problems: social phobia, panic and agoraphobia and "double depression" (chronic mild to moderate depression interspersed with episodes of major depression).

panic and agoraphobia. Only her additions are shown here. In each individual story, an omitted letter means they did not have anything more to add to that coping skill.

Kirsten's Additions to the ABCS

A: "I need to accept that I have panic and agoraphobia, social anxiety and depression and that it will probably take many months to get better."

C: "I need to remind myself that I have never thrown up in public and if I ever do it will probably be because I am sick – not just stressed."

S: "My boyfriend and I will celebrate when I finish my personal commitments to go out."

Kirsten experienced many ups and downs, but she continued to use her ABCS to help her make progress. She first found a part-time job but later found a full-time position in a large corporation. She also became more confident in non-work social situations such as parties and sporting activities. Her depression had lifted and her panic attacks and agoraphobia were no longer a problem.[3] She continued to use the ABCS to cope with her remaining social anxiety. Occasionally she would bring in an incident log so we could focus on healthy countering of the thoughts that upset her. Over time she was able to do more and more of this work for herself. I understand that since successfully concluding therapy she met a new boyfriend and they subsequently married. She now has a child and has continued her professional career.

---

3   By this time her scores on the BDI and the MI were no longer in the clinical range, supporting this fact. Her SPIN score was much better, but not yet in the "normal" range. She agreed to go into the follow-up phase and her sessions were scheduled less and less often. After another year of continued work, with visits every month or two, her SPIN score fell into the "normal" range and she felt increasingly confident.

Social Anxiety

The core fear of social anxiety is that the individual will make a mistake, or that others will notice their symptoms of stress, and that they will then be judged negatively and such a situation would be totally overwhelming. Sometimes, this involves a special fear of any conflict – no matter how small. The individual may want to avoid being the center of attention and so may avoid speaking up in a group situation. Some individuals may have a special fear of performing in front of others. Some individuals may not want to ever voice their opinion. Others may have a persistent belief that despite any of their accomplishments, deep down they are frauds. If you recognize any of these behaviors in yourself, you may be experiencing social anxiety.

Specific types of other people may elicit a bigger fear response. For some people, their peers may elicit the most fear. For others, older, well-dressed strangers are especially troubling. However, the core fear for everyone who experiences social anxiety is the dread of being judged negatively by others.

One special aspect of social anxiety is the tendency to compare oneself to others in an unrealistic manner. Earlier I referred to this as "comparisonitus." This means that the individual with social anxiety jumps to conclusions about others who they perceive as being brilliant, gorgeous, wealthy and without any flaws. A typical story goes like this: "I pulled up at the traffic light and in the car next to me was a handsome, well-dressed man and his beautiful wife. In the back seat were two beautiful, well-behaved young children. The car was the type of convertible I have always wanted. I thought to myself: I am such a loser compared to that man and his family." Of course, this individual has only a very superficial knowledge of the other man at the traffic light. The other man may be out on parole. His wife may be having an affair with someone else. The children in the back seat may be having serious problems at school. The point is, there is often very little evidence to support these kinds of snap-judgment comparisons with others. The only person's life story we know extremely well is our own (and as you have learned, even your own life story can be distorted with unrealistic thinking). Therefore, we need to focus on those things we can control and learn to make better choices about our own behavior rather than making meaningless comparisons with others.

The ABCS for Coping with Social Anxiety

A is for acceptance of all things you cannot control. Our human nature doesn't allow us to control our own emotions and the automatic thoughts that sometimes pop into our minds, like "I always act like a fool," or "I'm not as competent as others." Our human nature also does not allow us to control what others think or do. In particular, don't get mad at yourself for feeling anxious in front of others. Acceptance means letting go of things you cannot control so you can focus on things you can do something about, like what you do and say and what choices you make in the present moment (e.g., choosing to use the ABCS when you have social anxiety). Choosing to voluntarily face unrealistic fears is the best way to reduce them. So once you have done your best to act assertively you need to learn to let it go and accept that you don't control it all. Acceptance can have a very positive influence on your social anxiety and fear.

B is for breathing slowly and naturally while you relax your muscle tension. So, when you get anxious in a social situation choose to breathe in a slow and natural manner and make sure you breathe out as much as you breathe in. As you breathe out, let go of muscle tension throughout your whole body. You can take charge of your breathing and your muscle tension and, if you do, you will provide a positive influence on your social anxiety.

C is for countering. "I always act like a fool," can be countered with: "Everyone makes mistakes − not just me." "Other people will judge me and think I am an idiot," can be countered with: "I cannot control or even know what others think of me so I need to do what I think is right and then let it go." "I can't stand it if others notice that I have a symptom of anxiety," can be countered with: "I cannot control what others notice. I need to let that go." Countering unrealistic thoughts with thoughts based on evidence and logic can have a positive influence on your social anxiety.

S is for staying with it. Once you have picked a feared social situation to face, stay with it until you have finished your personal time commitment. While you are there focus on what the other people are saying and respond to them. Over time, staying with it can build your confidence in facing situations that have produced social anxiety.

Pete's Story

In our first therapy session, Pete's eyes teared up when he described how social anxiety had limited his life since he was in elementary school. He is a handsome young man, but in that first session he had his winter hat pulled down so far it hid half of his face. He told me that as a college student he had told his doctor about his problem and had been prescribed a medication that sometimes helps with anxiety and depression. Pete had been taking the anti-depressant for years, with only minimal gains. Now he was married and had three young children, but was working part-time in a menial job even though he had a college education and had once had high hopes for a career. When his first child came along he had volunteered to be the stay at home parent, partly due to his social anxiety. He felt trapped and was becoming increasingly depressed. At this point he seldom left the house and had almost no social life. When faced with a social situation that he couldn't avoid, he reported feeling that others noticed his discomfort and judged him.[4]

Pete was introduced to the ABCS for coping with social anxiety and he haltingly began to use these coping skills. We developed

---

4   Based on interviews and also on symptom questionnaires such as SPIN and BDI it became clear that he suffered from two primary issues: social phobia and dysthymic disorder (chronic depression). His social anxiety score was in the severe range and his depression score was in the moderate range. From his reports it seemed likely that the social anxiety had become more and more debilitating and that as a consequence he had become depressed as well.

some realistic personal goals and he began to also use the Ten Rules for Coping with Depression (see Chapter 5). He began to see that the coping skills were having a positive influence on his life. It also came to light that he had experienced an emotionally traumatic and embarrassing event in elementary school, which still troubled him. We revised his ABCS and began to go over and over his memories of this event until he was able to tell the story with much less fear and upset. His willingness to expose himself to these memories eventually resulted in him feeling better about the memories and this gave him additional motivation to change. He began to understand the need to accept all things not in his control and he began to make personal commitments to go out more and stay in social situations. He also began to practice being assertive. His use of countering improved and he began to bring in incident logs based on stressful encounters he had experienced. We reviewed and made changes to the logs so he could learn to better use the ABCS when the next stressful situation occurred.

Pete's Additions to the ABCS

A: "I need to accept that I have social anxiety and depression, and that I have PTSD symptoms related to a past trauma."

B: "I need to use brief relaxation before I enter new social situations."

C: "I need to remind myself that I am not a child in elementary school anymore. I am an adult who can cope with tough situations."

S: "My wife and I have agreed to celebrate whenever I finish a personal commitment to face a new social situation."

In time, we reviewed Pete's ups and downs and he began to see that even though there would be many more challenges ahead, he could really get somewhere with long-term effort.[5] He applied for a better job at his workplace and was promoted. He was going out

---

5   After six or seven months of treatment, focused on use of the ABCS, we discussed going into the follow-up phase. We reviewed his repeat SPIN and BDI scores, which documented that he had indeed made some significant improvement. He

with his wife and other couples on a frequent basis. We discussed future challenges and he felt optimistic and able to use his coping skills going forward.

GAD

The core fear for GAD is that some event will occur that is catastrophic in nature: this may be the death or injury of a family member, the onset of a life threatening disease or a financial catastrophe such as losing a job and never finding another one. The actual chances of the event occurring in the immediate future are in reality quite low and the chances of these events happening in succession are even more unlikely. However, when the individual is caught up in the worry the perceived likelihood of a catastrophe or series of catastrophes is exaggerated.

It is a part of human nature to worry about potential problems that may occur in the future. Worry can be helpful, if it involves something that is in our control. For example, imagine a college student who has a major test coming up. As the test approaches the student may begin to have occasional worry thoughts because they know they need to do well. However, a few days before the test, the student may still be going out with friends or playing video games rather than studying. When the worry gets more intense, the student then begins to focus on study and pretty soon the worry begins to subside. The student's worry served a useful purpose – to motivate getting the study done.

On the other hand we sometimes worry about situations we have no real control over, in which we cannot really do anything about the likelihood of a catastrophe. Imagine a parent whose grown-up child has a busy career that involves flying from city to city. The

---

reported that he was feeling more confident in using the coping skills and so follow-up began. Sessions were now scheduled every two to three weeks. When he came in for a session he sometimes brought in a partially or fully completed incident log. In time, his scores and reports all showed that he was functioning in the "normal" range.

parent, who suffers with GAD, may have hours of high stress when their child is flying. They may be preoccupied and not able to focus on normal activities during these times. They may have trouble sleeping. The parent may also come into conflict with their child because they urge them to fly less often or call home repeatedly during their travels. However, the parent can't simply order their child to quit this job. All of the worry, stress and misery the parent experiences does not make their offspring one bit safer: in fact it may make them unhappy too.

GAD worries are usually about something that the sufferer cannot really control. In addition, there is often a tendency to compulsively check that the catastrophe hasn't happened. Finally, there is a disruption to daily activities and also a disruption in relaxation and sleep. There may also be a disruption in relationships.

A story may help to illustrate how GAD works and what can be done about it. Many hundreds of years ago in Japan an old peasant with a white beard lived with his family. All of his life he had wanted to make a pilgrimage to his home temple on the slopes of Mount Fuji. One day he made up his mind and began to pack for the long journey. Japan was covered with a network of footpaths but the old man did not have a map. On clear days he could see the snow-covered top of Mount Fuji on the distant horizon. So, when he came to a fork in the trail he planned to simply take the path that seemed to lead him closer to the mountain. The old peasant said his goodbyes and set out on his journey. At first, he walked along at a good pace and as he walked he enjoyed the sounds of the birds singing and the sight of the beautiful flowering plants along the trail. Whenever he met a fellow walker they exchanged friendly words and sometimes shared a meal. He kept following the paths that he thought would lead toward Mount Fuji.

As the days and weeks of his journey passed the old peasant began to stare at Mount Fuji more and more often. Because he was looking at the mountaintop, he was not noticing the rocks and tree roots along the trail. As a result, he began to stumble frequently. He began to think: "An old man like me can never walk to Mount Fuji." "I will probably be attacked by wild animals when I walk through the for-est." "I will drown when I have to cross a river." "When I walk past a village, ruffians will beat me up and steal my food and leave me for dead." "Mount Fuji is so very far away." He was becoming more and more dispirited and appeared increasingly fragile. His clothing was dirty and his feet were bruised and bleeding from his many falls.

One day, as the old peasant crept along the trail through the foothills of Mount Fuji, a young farmer was plowing his field with his ox. The farmer looked down to the trail just in time to see the old peasant falter and then fall. The farmer rushed down to help. He picked the old peasant up and took him back to his home, gave him all he could eat and offered him a bed for the night. The next morning the young farmer asked the old peasant a series of questions. The purpose of the questions was to see if the old man could make sense of what had gone wrong on his journey. After many patient questions, at last the old man said:

"Now I know what went wrong and what I need to do about it. I slowly began to obsess about how far away Mount Fuji was and how I had no chance of finishing the journey. I distressed myself more and more with all the catastrophes that I could imagine. After a while, I focused all my attention on these thoughts and on the distant moun-tain and forgot to watch where I took my next step, and so I began

to stumble and fall. I started to dread the rest of the journey and wanted to give up.

"Now, I want to continue my journey, but I will teach myself to only deal with problems when, and if, they arise. I will keep my eyes on the path ahead and be ready to appreciate and enjoy the rest of my journey."

The ABCS for Coping with GAD

A is for acceptance of all things you cannot control. Accept that life has uncertainty and risk. We cannot control what others think or do or protect ourselves, or our loved ones, from all harm. Compulsive checking will feed the excessive worry. Acceptance means letting go of things you cannot control so you can focus on things you can do something about, like what you do and say and what choices you make, in the present moment (e.g., using coping skills like the ABCS). If you have a good understanding of human nature you also know that choosing to voluntarily face unrealistic worries and fears is the best way to reduce them. Once you have done your best to face your fears while using your coping skills, you need to learn to let it go. Acceptance of all this can have a positive influence on your worries.

B is for breathing slowly and naturally while you relax your muscle tension. You can take charge of your breathing and muscle tension, and provide a positive influence on your anxiety and worry.

C is for countering your worry with the truth. Remind yourself to consider the actual evidence and logic without jumping to conclusions. Remember that the chances of a real catastrophe are much less than you think. Worries are not the same as the events you fear. "If my boss doesn't smile at me today, that means I will be fired, never find another job, become homeless and die alone on the street!" can be countered with: "If my boss didn't smile that could be because he has indigestion or because he had a fight with his wife. The chances of all these catastrophes happening one after the other are very low." Remind yourself that you cannot protect others from all harm, no matter how much you worry. For example, "My adult son will be killed while traveling," can be countered with: "The evidence shows that flying is really quite safe and I need to let this thought go because it is not in my control." Remind yourself that you will only deal with catastrophes when, or if, they ever happen. Countering can have a positive influence on worry.

S is for staying with the ABCS to help you face this worry (and your fear) without repeatedly checking for reassurance. So, after you have acted prudently, you need to let it go without repeatedly checking for reassurance. Excessive checking wastes hours of your time and usually upsets the person you are checking on. Since checking also maintains worries, try postponing your extra checking and get involved in something else. This is a positive use of distraction techniques. Make a commitment to face your worries once a day and otherwise try to let them go.

OCD

Obsessions are often triggered by situations that pop up in everyday life, and different individuals will experience different types of obsessive thoughts and fears. Perhaps the most common obsession is that the individual will become contaminated with germs or toxins. The core fear in this case may be that the individual will become ill and die, or that they will unknowingly contaminate others who will then become ill or die. The individual may spend lots of time avoiding objects that they think may be contaminated. This individual may spend even more time doing compulsive cleaning, washing and checking to try to feel some relief.

The core fear underlying one type of severe aggressive obsession is the invasive thought that the individual will either self-harm or hurt someone else (either physically or emotionally). The individual fears that this will happen either accidentally or voluntarily if they "lose control." Invasive thoughts could include: "I could stab my mother." "I could hurt my child." "I could jump off that cliff." The individual feels horrified by the thought and performs compulsive checks for reassurance that the feared action is not really happening. They may also avoid situations in which they fear something bad might happen. Individuals who are diagnosed with this type of OCD are very unlikely to actually do harm to others.

Please note: as mentioned earlier, if you experience this type of aggressive obsession you need to immediately seek a mental health evaluation.

Other obsessions may not involve fear, but instead a feeling of discomfort that arises when the individual encounters objects that are not in the "correct order" or are arranged in a manner that is not symmetrical. Some individuals with OCD must make their own touches match. For example, "If I touch a pencil three times with my right hand, I must touch it three times with my left." Physically arranging objects or actions exactly in order is the compulsion for this type of obsession.

There are many different types of obsession, but regardless of the type, some individuals have one primary obsession and accompanying compulsions, while other individuals may have several different sets of obsessions with accompanying compulsions. Sometimes the obsession, or obsessions, may remain the same for many years. For other individuals, the type of obsession may vary from time to time. Obsessions and compulsions may consume hours of time each day.

Use the version of the ABCS that follows to seek out opportunities to face your fears, without performing compulsions. It is more manageable to take on one situation at a time rather than everything at once. Recovery comes from your choice to repeatedly face your fears (without compulsions), as you use your coping skills.

The ABCS for Coping with OCD

A is for acceptance of all things you cannot control. Accept that life has uncertainty and risk. Obsessions are often triggered by situations that pop up in everyday life. Accept that you do have OCD and the best way to reduce it is to stop avoiding situations and stop compulsive behaviors, in a step-by-step manner. By definition an obsession is based on an unrealistic fear. Obsessive thoughts are not the same as the event you fear. Thoughts alone do not produce catastrophes. When you obsess, the actual chances of a real catastrophe are much less than you think. Accept that you cannot protect yourself or your loved ones from all harm. No one has that kind of power. So, once you have done your best to face your fears while using your coping skills, you need to learn to let it go.

B is for breathing slowly and naturally. You can take charge of your breathing and your muscle tension and, if you do, you will provide a positive influence on how you are feeling when you have an obsessive thought.

C is for countering your obsession with the truth: "This is an obsession."

S is for staying with it. Don't avoid "triggers," instead learn to face the obsessional fear without performing any compulsions. Once you have faced the fear then try to get involved in some other activity: use a positive distraction. At first, you may try to postpone the compulsion and busy yourself with something else. For example, tell yourself: "I'll call a friend and we'll talk for a few minutes and then when the call is finished maybe the compulsive urge won't be so strong." When the time is up, if you are still caught up in the obsession, try postponing again. If you slip and start performing the compulsion, then do it differently or for a shorter amount of time. If you are still having trouble, try to step back from the situation and consider the negative long-term effects on your obsession if you "feed it" by performing yet another compulsion. Building self-control is hard work, but self-control can be strengthened.[6] Work toward the end goal of not avoiding "triggers" and not acting out compulsions. Make a commitment to face your fears in a step-by-step manner: one situation at a time.

Please keep in mind that if you try to avoid a situation or perform checks over and over again for reassurance, you can make it worse by "feeding the obsession." You need to tolerate the fear and postpone, then eventually eliminate, any compulsive checking or reassuring. Also, don't turn the ABCS into a compulsion by trying to use them perfectly before you face a trigger.

Franklin's Story

Franklin was a thin man in his mid-forties who seemed to be consumed by worry and fear. He came to me for treatment because of his continued jealousy over his wife's letters from "an old flame" whom she had dated many years before. Even though the letters had been sent prior to their marriage, Franklin was unable to let it go. He felt compelled to question her repeatedly about her old relationship – which often resulted in a major argument. Several nights a week Franklin would lie in bed for hours tossing and turning and obsessing about this problem. Franklin had been active in Alcoholics Anonymous until a few years ago and credited AA with making his recovery possible. (He had abused alcohol from his late teens to early twenties, "because I couldn't handle the stresses of life.") When he began therapy, he hadn't had a drink in over 20 years. However, he told me he was starting to have more frequent urges to drink. He had always been a worrier. He had vivid memories of himself aged 13, staring out the window and worrying about his younger sister if she was late coming home from school. Even when his parents told him there was no need to worry he couldn't let it go. In his adult life, Franklin found that he worried excessively whenever his adult son brought the grandchildren to visit. He couldn't enjoy the visit because of the fear that the kids would run into the street or get injured somehow. He constantly checked to see if they were okay. Additionally, ever since an old family friend had experienced a

---

6   See the work of Mischel (2014) for more information.

debilitating stroke, Franklin couldn't get it out of his mind that he was going to have a stroke too, because he was so stressed out by worry. He checked his own pulse repeatedly throughout the day and had visited his doctor frequently, even though the doctor always reassured him that he was physically healthy. Franklin told me that he didn't think of himself as being depressed, but all these thoughts interfered with his happiness.[7]

His obsessive fears drove a variety of compulsive behaviors designed to check for reassurance. Sometimes his checking on other family members resulted in family conflict. He also suffered from mild, but chronic, clinical depression.

Franklin began to use the ABCS for coping with OCD to help him deal with his jealousy and anger toward his wife. He also learned to use the STOP technique (see Chapter 6) to assist him in reducing his angry questioning. I also encouraged him to resume his participation in AA meetings and reminded him that using alcohol to escape his negative emotions would block all chances of progress. He was able to follow through with AA successfully. He learned to appreciate that his wife had chosen him, despite any other relationships she had had in her life. He also learned to accept the uncertainty and risk that is an inherent part of life. He learned to counter his unhealthy thoughts and to stay with his commitment to reduce, and then eliminate, his compulsive questioning of his wife. Over time his marriage improved and he used the ABCS to cope with other areas of concern, such as his fears about his own health and the safety of his grandchildren.

---

7   Interviews and clinical questionnaires such as the Yale-Brown Obsessive Compulsive Scale Checklist (YBOCS Checklist), the Yale-Brown Obsessive Compulsive Scale (YBOCS) and the BDI revealed that Franklin suffered from a form of OCD that was expressed through obsessing about his marital relationship, the safety of his grandchildren and his own health. If he obsessed exclusively about his health then the proper diagnosis might have been illness anxiety, but Franklin obsessed about a variety of issues and some of them had nothing to do with his health.

Franklin's Additions to the ABCS

A: "I need to let the past go. I need to accept that I have a problem with jealousy and anger. I am an alcoholic and need to stay clean and sober. I need to accept that I have OCD with jealousy and illness anxiety and also depression."

B: "When I feel jealous I need to use the STOP technique and brief relaxation."

C: "I need to remind myself that my wife has chosen me rather than leaving me for someone else."

Over the next year or so Franklin gradually improved by using the ABCS.[8] When he was ready to finish therapy, we discussed the continued importance of using his coping skills whenever they were needed in the future.

Illness Anxiety

The core fear of illness anxiety is that some ache, pain or blemish is a sign or symptom of a catastrophic and fatal illness. Individuals who suffer with this disorder feel almost certain that they have the illness, despite a lack of any real evidence, sometimes even when their doctor tells them otherwise. Individuals with this disorder are not faking it. They strongly believe that they have the illness and feel all the emotions that go along with such a diagnosis. They often perform frequent checks in an attempt to gain reassurance, but any reassurance is very temporary. An individual might make too frequent trips to the doctor; alternatively they might avoid even routine visits because of the fear of having the illness

---

8   With improvement in his anxiety disorder, his mood improved and his scores on the YBOCS and the BDI all fell into the "normal" range. We agreed to move his case into follow-up and we gradually reduced the frequency of visits until he was only seen for a consultation every few months. After two years of treatment we agreed to close the case, since his scores were all maintaining in the "normal" range and he continued to function well.

officially confirmed. Illness anxiety is very similar to GAD or OCD except the primary focus is on physical well-being.

Use the version of the ABCS that follows to seek out opportunities to face your fears, without performing compulsive checks. It is more manageable to take on one situation at a time rather than everything at once. Recovery comes from your choice to repeatedly face your fears without compulsive checking, as you use your coping skills.

The ABCS for Coping with Illness Anxiety

A is for acceptance of all things you cannot control. Accept that life has uncertainty and risk. Our human nature doesn't allow us to control worry thoughts about health that pop into our minds. Our human nature does not allow us to protect ourselves from all harm. You may have some influence with some of these things, but you do not have complete control. If you have a health concern all you can do is eat healthy foods, exercise and maintain a healthy lifestyle. You can find a good doctor and then follow your doctor's advice. Worrying about things that you cannot control is fruitless. Choosing to voluntarily face unrealistic fears is the best way to reduce them. So once you have acted prudently you need to let it go without repeatedly checking for reassurance.

B is for breathing slowly and naturally while you relax your muscle tension. You can take charge of your breathing and muscle tension, and provide a positive influence on your illness anxiety.

C is for countering your worries with the truth. Remind yourself to consider the evidence, in a logical way, without jumping to conclusions. Remember that the actual chances of experiencing a real, catastrophic illness in the immediate future are much less than you think. Worries are not the same as the events you fear. For example: "If I have a blemish on my back that means I have a fatal skin cancer," can be countered with: "If I have a blemish that doesn't mean it must be skin cancer and if I did have skin cancer that doesn't mean it would be fatal. My next visit to my doctor is only a few weeks away and I can ask about it then." Remind yourself that you cannot protect yourself from all uncertainty or harm, no matter how much you worry. Remind yourself that you will deal with catastrophes only if and when they happen. Countering unrealistic thoughts with thoughts based on evidence and logic can have a positive influence on illness anxiety.

S is for staying with it. Face this worry without repeatedly checking for reassurance. Excessive checking wastes hours of your time. At first, try postponing your extra checking and busy yourself with something else. Use distraction constructively. When the time is up if you are still caught by the worry, try postponing again. Work toward the end goal of not doing any excessive checking.

PTSD

The core fear of PTSD is that the individual cannot accept their memories of trauma because they are so upsetting. A related belief often held by PTSD sufferers is that they must not be "weak" and that means never experiencing strong, negative emotions. As a result, they try to block out trauma memories and feared emotions, but in so doing also block the chance of recovery. Recovery requires using coping skills to repeatedly face the trauma memories.

Please note: if you think you have PTSD you need to find a therapist to help you with your treatment. The version of the ABCS that follows shows how cognitive behavioral therapists begin to work with patients who have PTSD. I do not advise using this without professional supervision. If you live in the USA, use the resources list to help find a mental health professional. If you are a veteran, you could also contact the Veterans Health Administration (https://www.va.gov/

health/): the organization has reorganized and improved the services provided to veterans with PTSD.

The ABCS for Coping with PTSD

A is for acceptance of all things you cannot control, including your memories of trauma that happened in the past and the raw emotions that are attached to those memories. Accept that life has uncertainty and risk. Our human nature doesn't allow us to control everything that happens to others or ourselves. Likewise, you can't block out all things that might trigger your trauma memories. If you talk about your memories in detail in an accepting, therapeutic environment you can become less fearful of your memories.

B is for taking charge of your breathing and muscle tension, providing a positive influence on how you feel when your memories of trauma are triggered.

C is for countering your memories of trauma with the truth. Remind yourself to consider the actual evidence and logic without jumping to conclusions or taking responsibility for things you can't control, or things you couldn't have known at the time of the trauma. Remember that memories are not the same as the past events you fear. You are in a different place now. Remind yourself that you cannot protect others from all harm, no matter how much you may have tried. For example: "I can't stand remembering what happened!" can be countered with: "I need to find a way to face my memories until I can cope with them." "I shouldn't be here," can be countered with: "For whatever reason, I am alive, therefore it is my responsibility to face my memories and move on with my life." Countering unrealistic thoughts with thoughts based on evidence and logic can have a positive influence on how you feel about your memories.

S is for staying with it by learning to talk about your memories with a mental health professional that you trust. Talk about each episode of trauma as you use your coping skills, until the memories don't frighten you so much. Continue with the same memory until the fear is greatly reduced, before moving on to the next one.

Susan's Story

Susan's husband accompanied her to her first therapy session. She had retired three years ago and had looked forward to having an active retirement with lots of time to travel and see her grandchildren. She was very composed until she related what had happened to her two and a half years ago. She was in a terrible car accident when another driver ran a traffic light. The other car had children in the back seat, who screamed and cried after the accident. The driver of the other car and one of the children in the back seat died at the scene. Susan had to spend several weeks in the hospital recuperating from broken bones and severe lacerations. Within a few months, she had made a full recovery from her injuries but continued to suffer with vivid nightmares about the car accident, several nights a week. Certain sights and sounds in everyday life triggered flashbacks. Susan would have a memory of the accident that was so real that she experienced the terror she had felt when the accident happened and she would tremble and perspire. Susan had given up driving and had trouble even sitting in the passenger seat of a car. When her husband drove she was very jittery and would frequently ask him to slow down. Since the accident, loud noises and the smell of gasoline made her jump and sometimes triggered flashbacks. Susan was upset with herself whenever these things happened and she tried to avoid all things that reminded her of the accident. Increasingly she avoided going out at all. She broke down when she described how limited her life had become since the accident.

Many years earlier, when she was a young adult and first establishing a life of her own, Susan had had some problems with what sounded like panic attacks. After she found her first job and became more settled the panic attacks had stopped and she had not experienced any other emotional problems until after the car accident, which had triggered her PTSD, and also panic and ago-raphobia.[9] During therapy, Susan began to learn how her avoidance of these memories was understandable, but was under-mining her desire to heal from this emotional trauma.

Susan's Additions to the ABCS

A: "I need to accept that I have both PTSD and symptoms of panic and agoraphobia."

B: "When I feel stress, don't hold my breath! Do brief relaxation."

C: "I am not responsible for the actions of the other driver."

S: "I can never run away from my own memories so I guess I will have to face them."

After the assessment was completed and by the fourth session, Susan was encouraged to perform the brief relaxation breathing technique for several minutes and then tell the story about the accident. Initially, it was hard to tell because the memories were so upsetting to her. The emotional trauma seemed to center on the scene of the accident: her vivid memories of the children screaming and also of the smell of gasoline (she was terrified that the car would catch on fire). After she told the story, she repeated the relaxation technique and then we did a debriefing. During that time she was encouraged to counter some of the unrealistic thoughts she had developed about the accident. By the end of the session she was emotionally exhausted, but had taken a huge step in acceptance by facing her memories. After about seven therapy sessions, and after the third retelling of the story, no more new memories of the accident came to her and so we made an audio recording of her story, complete with the relaxation and the debriefing. She was encouraged to play the recording once a day between sessions. Shortly after that, she began to feel much less frightened and upset by her memories and reported that she had started to drive again. By the tenth therapy session and the sixth

---

9 Both interviews and clinical questionnaires, such as the Modified PTSD Symptom Scale Self-Report (MPSS-SR), confirmed this.

retelling of the story in our therapy sessions, the memories were no longer terrifying to her. She reported that although she would never like talking about it, she was no longer afraid to do so and she had even talked to her husband and a close friend about the accident. We had two more follow-up sessions, each about six weeks apart and Susan and her husband continued to report that she was still driving and able to go out and that the triggers which had caused flashbacks and panic were no longer causing trouble.

Specific Phobia

The object and core fear of a specific phobia varies from one individual to another. Typically, these core fears are all connected to dangers faced in our human history. We have evolved to be alert to situations that may present real danger. Common phobias include fear of heights, fear of animals with large teeth, fear of thunderstorms, fear of the dark, fear of injury and blood and fear of spiders or snakes. For our ancestors, these fears may have served a useful evolutionary purpose, but for us they are less helpful.

There are too many different phobias to adapt the ABCS for each one here. However, the following ABCS can easily be tailored to your particular phobia. However, there is a notable exception. Blood-injection-injury phobia can cause the sufferer to feel faint or to actually faint. If an individual faints and strikes their head on a hard surface they could be concussed. A different technique must be used if an individual with blood-injection-injury phobia feels faint, and this will require a medical consultation and treatment by a cognitive behavioral psychologist or therapist who is experienced in treatment of this type of phobia.[10]

---

10 This alternate technique is called Applied Tension and was developed and described by Ost and Sterner (1987). The Applied Tension technique allows you to counteract the tendency to faint through selective use of muscle tension.

The ABCS for Coping with Specific Phobias

A is for acceptance of all things you cannot control. No one can control whether they develop a phobia at some point in their life. If you have a good understanding of human nature you also know that choosing to voluntarily face unrealistic fears is the best way to reduce them.

B is for taking charge of your breathing and your muscle tension. If you do, you will provide a positive influence on how you are feeling when you face your phobic situation.

C is for countering unrealistic thoughts with thoughts based on evidence and logic, which can have a positive influence on how you feel when you face your phobia. For example: "I know I am going to be injured or killed!" can be countered with: "The evidence shows that there is little risk."

S is for staying with it to take on your fears in a step-by-step manner. Once you have picked a feared situation to face, stay with it until you have finished your commitment. You can break down your phobic fear into smaller steps and then begin to face it.

Problems with Adjusting to Negative Life Changes

Sometimes in life, challenges occur that are difficult to cope with. We might experience losses of varying kinds: for example, divorce or the end of a relationship, or the death of a spouse, a family member or a close friend. Other losses may include losing a job, failing to get into a favored college or, in later life, being forced to give up a driver's license or having to give up living in the

---

Details of the article are in the bibliography should you be interested in reading more. Another good reference point is Chapter 14 of Abramowitz, Deacon and Whiteside's *Exposure Therapy for Anxiety* (2011). If you think you may have this particular phobia, use the resources list to find a mental health professional who can help you with this alternate technique.

family home to move into a senior living facility. In addition, sometimes we may face negative life changes, such as getting a new, difficult boss or discovering that we, or a family member or friend, have a serious medical problem. For some individuals these negative life changes may result in disruptive levels of stress and anxiety that interfere with their normal daily functioning.

Since everyone is different and negative life changes may trigger different core fears, I have provided two examples that illustrate how the ABCS may be adapted to deal with these types of situations.

Andrew's Story: Dealing with a Difficult, Demanding Boss

Andrew was a high achiever, but also a worrier, who was middle-aged and had a wife and an 18-year-old daughter. Andrew had worked in the same organization for many years and was seen as being very capable. Recently, Andrew's boss had retired and had been replaced by a new one who seldom gave positive feedback and who seemed to be more concerned with his own status in the organization than with building an effective team.

Andrew's core fear was that his new boss did not value his past achievements or future potential, and might even demote or fire him. If this happened then Andrew would lose some of the respect that he had earned from others. Losing his wage or taking a pay cut might also mean he'd have trouble funding his daughter's college education. As a result of these fears, Andrew frequently worried about losing respect and losing his ability to pay his daughter's college bills. Whenever he was not directly engaged in some activity, he became increasingly preoccupied with his worries. Andrew started to have trouble falling asleep at night and sometimes tossed and turned for several hours before falling asleep. After a few weeks of Andrew being preoccupied in this way, his wife told him that he complained too much about his work situation and had become less involved with their family. She said that Andrew "dumped" all his negativity on her when he got home from work. It was at this point that he realized his feelings about work were negatively affecting his home life, and he decided to seek help in dealing with his worries.

The ABCS for Coping with Worries Like Andrew's

A is for acceptance of all things you cannot control, including the hiring of a new boss and what that new boss thinks or does.

B is for breathing slowly and relaxing muscle tension whenever worry about the work situation occurs.

C is for countering unhealthy and unrealistic thoughts. For example: "I will be demoted or fired," can be countered with: "My boss hasn't said anything to me about being demoted or fired. I don't have any real evidence that this will happen. But in the unlikely event that I did get fired, I could work hard and consistently at applying for new jobs and probably find something, eventually." "I will lose the respect of my co-workers, my friends and my family," can be countered with: "My co-workers and friends know me well and most won't change their views of me because of a difficult boss's decisions. My family loves me and I have no reason to believe that that will change because of my boss's decisions." "If I can't pay for my daughter's college education that means I am a bad father," can be countered with: "Even if I were demoted or fired I could still eventually get another job and pay some of my daughter's tuition. It doesn't make me a bad father just because I have less money. I am responsible for what I do, not what others do. I am jumping to conclusions about all of this."

S is for staying with it. Once a day, find a quiet place and set aside 10 to 15 minutes to confront each worry thought directly. Hold it in mind for a few moments and then counter it. When this is done, use the breathing and relaxing coping skill to let it go and then get back to normal life. At all other times of the day, focus attention on the people you are with and the activities you are involved in. When you have worry thoughts at other times of the day, let them go by telling yourself you will deal with them only once a day and now is a time to refocus on the people around you and the activity you are engaged in.

After six therapy sessions Andrew had learned to use the ABCS and to confront and counter his fears and his worry in the session. Shortly thereafter he began to do these worry management sessions at home on a daily basis. He reported that he was increasingly able to get into conversations and activities more fully. After about ten sessions we decided to schedule one more follow-up session a month later. At that session he reported that his wife had told him that she was glad he was no longer complaining so much about his work and glad to have him "back in the family."

Kathy's Story: Dealing with the Loss of an Important Relationship

Kathy was in her mid-twenties and was newly single. She had recently graduated from college after six years of part-time study combined with part-time work as a clerk. Kathy's parents had divorced when she was in her teens and both her mother and father had remarried, resulting in their attention being diverted to their new families and away from her. She was not very close with either parent, although she talked to her mother about once a week. She found this emotional distance from her parents upsetting. Kathy said that she had several close friends and that her employer wanted to promote her now that she had graduated. Until recently, she had been dating Pat, who she had met in her first year of college and fallen in love with. The relationship progressed and by her last year in college they had begun to talk about marriage. However, as graduation approached, Pat announced that he was planning to accept a job in another city and was just not ready to settle down and get married.

Kathy's core fear was that she would be alone for the rest of her life. She feared she would never meet anyone else she could fall in love with and she would become a sort of "hermit."

The ABCS for Coping with Loss Like Kathy's

A is for acceptance of things not in your control, including other people's decisions.

B is for breathing slowly and relaxing muscle tension when worry about being alone occurs.

C is for countering unhealthy, unrealistic thoughts. "I will become a sort of hermit; always alone," can be countered with: "I have close friends and that shows that I can maintain relationships. I can't control what my parents or Pat did, but I can choose to see my friends and get on with my work. No one can totally control the future, but if I stay active I will meet new people and may even fall in love again someday."

S is for staying with it. Confront worry thoughts and fears by countering them. Focus on staying active and connected rather than withdrawing.

After a few sessions, we developed the ABCS for Kathy and she began to work on using the coping skills. She began to counter her unhealthy thoughts and to accept that her behavior and her choices were under her control. She focused on keeping active and being a good friend. She also focused on doing well at work. Kathy had several ups and downs over the next few months, but she continued her efforts and after about four months we decided to schedule two more follow-up sessions each four to six weeks apart. At the last session Kathy laughed about her fears of being a hermit. She had started to date again and was doing well in her new job.

This chapter shows how core fears can be identified and how the ABCS can be adapted to fit each one. This includes fears that are typically part of anxiety disorders and phobias, as well as those fears that arise due to negative life changes. The stories from my clinical experience in this chapter demonstrate how individuals have successfully adapted the ABCS for their core fears. These stories also illustrate how frequently people suffer from multiple anxiety disorders and how often depression can accompany anxiety. Individuals may also experience problems coping with anger, and if so this needs to be addressed as well. This is why depression and anger and impulsivity formed the focus of the previous two chapters. Overall these stories demonstrate the importance of addressing all the emotional issues that an individual is experiencing; not just one. They also show that it is possible to make improvements by committing to face core fear(s) while using the coping skills. The exercise that follows is vital, because it allows you to put everything you have learned into practice!

Exercise

Fill in the blanks that follow to identify your own core fear(s) and develop your ABCS. In each section there is space for you to add information that will help make the ABCS specific to you. For example, if you are having trouble coping with a recent divorce or the diagnosis of a medical problem, then list it under A. Also, if you have a problem with depression, anger or other related issues, be sure to note it there. You may also find it helpful to circle or highlight any general points or examples that particularly apply to your situation as you read through the following sections. If you are seeing a psychologist or therapist, ask them to help you to complete this process.

My core fear(s):

_____

_____

_____

_____

My ABCS

A is for acceptance of all the things I cannot control. Although I am responsible for my own actions and for learning to use coping skills in the present moment, I accept my human nature and the many things that I cannot control, such as:

1.   The past.

2.   The fact that life has uncertainty and risk.

3.   The automatic thoughts that pop into my mind.

4.   My emotions and feelings.

5.   What others think and do.

6. Whether those I love are safe from all harm.

7. The fact that fears don't go away on their own (they must be faced).

8. The future.

Here is a list of anything else I need to accept:

_____

_____

_____

_____

_____

_____

Remember: while there are things that you can never completely control, taking charge of your behavior can allow you to have some positive influence on many of these things. This is especially the case for any problems you may have added that involve your behavior rather than your feelings.

ß is for breathing slowly and naturally while I relax my muscle tension. High levels of anxiety or panic often trigger rapid, shallow breathing (i.e., hyperventilation). Rapid, shallow breathing increases stress by reducing the amount of carbon dioxide in my blood so much that I can feel lightheaded. So, when I get anxious, I choose to breathe in a slow and natural manner and make sure I breathe out for as long as I breathe in. As I breathe out, I will let go of muscle tension throughout my whole body. I can take charge of my breathing and my muscle tension and if I do, I will provide a positive influence on how I am feeling.

Here is any other information that might help me with breathing and relaxing:

_____

_____

_____

_____

_____

C is for countering any unrealistic or catastrophic thoughts with the truth. For example:

"I can't stand feeling like this!" can be countered with: "I am learning to cope with these feelings."

"I shouldn't feel anxious!" can be countered with: "I need to accept that my emotions are not under my direct control."

"I shouldn't have a thought like this!" can be countered with: "This is an automatic thought and thoughts are not the same as actions."

"Other people will judge me and think I am an idiot!" can be countered with: "I cannot control or even know what others think of me so I need to do what I think is right and then let it go."

These are my own most difficult thoughts and the counters I will use to deal with them:

_____

_____

_____

_____

_____

_____

_____

_____

_____

Remember: countering unrealistic thoughts with thoughts based on evidence and logic can have a positive influence on how you feel.

S is for staying with it so I can fully face my unrealistic fears and anxieties until they are reduced. It means not escaping from or avoiding the situation, or getting temporary relief by using alcohol or drugs, or repeatedly checking for reassurance. It means fully being there as I voluntarily choose to face the fear. However, I don't have to face all my fears at once. I can take them on in a step-by-step manner. But once I have picked a feared situation to face, I will stay with it until I have finished my commitment.

What follows is any other information that will help motivate me to stay with it and face my fears:

_____

_____

_____

_____

_____

Congratulations on developing your own personalized ABCS for coping with anxiety and stress. Use it to help you remember to use healthy coping skills when you are facing your fears and whenever you encounter disruptive stress and anxiety in your daily life. It is important to remember that you will only improve by actively facing your fears.

CONCLUSION

As you are probably well aware, anxiety problems and the social stigma that is still wrongfully attached to them can make you feel alone – as if no one else in the world has these problems. Yet, as I outlined earlier in this book, it is actually the case that millions of people around the world have these same types of problems. Everyone has some anxiety some of the time. Problems with anxiety are a part of the human condition. However, throughout this book, you will have seen that the ABCS can be learned and used as coping skills to begin to reverse the negative effects of anxiety and stress. If you have completed the exercises throughout the book, you will have seen how the ABCS can be applied in your own life. It is common to experience related depression or anger alongside an anxiety disorder, so additional coping skills for dealing with these problems were presented in Chapters 5 and 6. Stories from my clinical experience, found throughout the book, have demonstrated how individuals who have faced combinations of these problems have successfully relied on the ABCS and other appropriate coping skills to address these issues. Of course, the coping skills need to be tailored to each individual and to their particular condition and life circumstances.

It is important to remember that the ABCS can be successfully used in a variety of situations; ranging from everyday stress and anxiety, to common fears and phobias, to classic anxiety disorders and finally to a combination of anxiety disorders along with related emotional problems. However, if you continue to have severe problems with anxiety or other emotional issues you need to seek the help of a cognitive behavioral therapist or another mental health professional who can help as you face your core fear(s) and as you apply coping skills like the ones described in this book. Seeking help when you need it is a sign of strength and wisdom; not a sign of weakness.

When I first started to focus on the treatment of anxiety a colleague of mine said that my professional choice would not be successful or rewarding because not enough people with anxiety disorders would be willing to face their own fears and work to overcome them. Thankfully, he was wrong and I have had the pleasure of working with many brave and inspiring patients over the years. I do know that people who suffer from anxiety demonstrate great courage when they choose to face their fears rather than try to ignore them. The fact that you have been willing to work through this book is an important first step in coping more effectively with your stress and anxiety. Well done!

Whether you work on your problems alone or with the help of a mental health professional, the journey will not be an easy one. However, as extensive research into CBT and my own 40 years of clinical experience demonstrate, it is possible to make good progress even when the road is long and hard and filled with many ups and downs. I want you to know that there is hope. I wish you well on your journey.

Resources

Anxiety and Depression Association of America (ADAA)
8701 Georgia Ave.
Suite 412
Silver Spring, MD 20910
Phone: 240-485-1001
Web site: www.adaa.org

Association for Behavioral and Cognitive Therapies (ABCT)
305 7th Avenue
16th Floor
New York, NY 10001
Phone: 212-647-1890
Web site: www.abct.org

International OCD Foundation, Inc. (IOCDF)
18 Tremont Street, Suite 308
Boston, MA 02108
Phone: 617-973-5801
Web site: www.ocfoundation.org

National Institute of Mental Health (NIMH)
Science Writing, Press, and Dissemination Branch
6001 Executive Blvd., Room 6200, MSC 9663
Bethesda, MD 20892-9663
Phone: 866-615-6464
Web site: www.nimh.nih.gov

Veterans Health Administration
U.S. Department of Veterans Affairs
810 Vermont Avenue, NW
Washington, DC 20420
Phone: 1-800-273-8255
Web site: www.va.gov/health/

Bibliography

Abramowitz, J.S., Deacon, B.J. and Whiteside, S.P.H. (2011). *Exposure Therapy for Anxiety: Principles and Practice.* New York, NY: The Guilford Press.

American Psychiatric Association (2013). *Diagnostic and Statistical Manual of Mental Disorders* (fifth edition). Arlington, VA: American Psychiatric Association Publishing.

Andrews, G., Creamer, M., Crino, R., Hunt, C., Lampe, L. and Page, A. (2003). *The Treatment of Anxiety Disorders: Clinician Guides and Patient Manuals* (second edition). Cambridge: Cambridge University Press.

Anthony, M.A., Orsillo, S.M. and Roemer, L. (eds.) (2001). *Practitioner's Guide to Empirically Based Measures of Anxiety.* New York, NY: Kluwer Academic/Plenum Publishers.

Aristotle, *Nicomachean Ethics*, in Knowles, E. (ed.) (2014). *Oxford Dictionary of Quotations.* Oxford: Oxford University Press.

Barlow, D.H. (2002). *Anxiety and its Disorders: The Nature and Treatment of Anxiety and Panic* (second edition). New York, NY: The Guilford Press.

Barlow, D.H., Ellard, K.K., Fairholme, C.P., Farchione, T.J., Boisseau, C.L., Ehrenreich-May, J.T. and Allen, L.B. (2011). *The Unified Protocol for Transdiagnostic Treatment of Emotional Disorders: Therapist Guide.* New York, NY: Oxford University Press.

Baxter, A.J., Scott, K.M., Vos, T. and Whiteford, H.A. (2013). Global prevalence of anxiety disorders: a systemic review and meta-regression, *Psychological Medicine*, (May) 43(5): 897–910.

Beck, A.T., Rush, A.J., Shaw, B.F. and Emery, G. (1979). *Cognitive Therapy of Depression.* New York, NY: The Guilford Press.

Beck, A.T., Ward, C.H., Mendelson, M., Mock, J. and Erbaugh, J. (1961). An inventory for measuring depression, *Archives of General Psychiatry*, 4(6): 561–571.

Benson, H. with Klipper, M.Z. (2000 [1975]). *The Relaxation Response.* New York, NY: HarperCollins.

Burns, D.D. (1980). *Feeling Good: The New Mood Therapy*. New York, NY: Avon Books.

Butler, A.C., Chapman, J.E., Forman, E.M. and Beck, A.T. (2006). The empirical status of cognitive-behavioral therapy: a review of meta-analyses, *Clinical Psychology Review*, (January) 26(1): 17–31.

Clark, D.M. (2011). Implementing NICE guidelines for the psychological treatment of depression and anxiety disorders: The IAPT experience, *International Review of Psychiatry*, (August) 23(4): 318–327.

Davidson, J.R.T. (ed.) (1998). *Social Anxiety Disorder*. Philadelphia, PA: Current Medicine, Inc.

Eifert, G.H. and Forsyth, J.P. (2005). *Acceptance and Commitment Therapy for Anxiety Disorders: A Practitioner's Treatment Guide to Using Mindfulness, Acceptance, and Values-Based Behavior Change Strategies*. Oakland, CA: New Harbinger.

Ellis, A. and Harper, R.A. (1961). *A Guide to Rational Living*. Englewood Cliffs, NJ: Prentice Hall.

Epictetus (1995). *The Art of Living: The Classic Manual on Virtue, Happiness, and Effectiveness*, Lebell, S. (tr.). San Francisco, CA: HarperCollins.

Foa, E.B. and Rothbaum, B.O. (1998). *Treating the Trauma of Rape: Cognitive-Behavioral Therapy for PTSD*. New York, NY: The Guilford Press.

Foa, E.B. and Wilson, R. (1991). *Stop Obsessing!: How to Overcome Your Obsessions and Compulsions*. New York, NY: Bantam.

Giles, L. (tr.) *Sayings of Lao-tzu,* in Speake, J. (ed.) (2008). *A Dictionary of Proverbs*. Oxford: Oxford University Press.

Hofmann, S.G. and Smits, J.A.J. (2008). Cognitive-behavioral therapy for adult anxiety disorders: a meta-analysis of randomized placebo-controlled trials, *Journal of Clinical Psychiatry*, (April) 69(4): 621–632.

Hope, D.A., Heimberg, R.G. and Turk, C.L. (2006). *Managing Social Anxiety: A Cognitive-Behavioral Therapy Approach: Therapist Guide*. New York, NY: Oxford University Press.

Hope, D.A., Heimberg, R.G. and Turk, C.L. (2010). *Managing Social Anxiety: A Cognitive-Behavioral Therapy Approach: Workbook* (second edition). New York, NY: Oxford University Press.

Jacobson, E. (1938). *Progressive Relaxation*. Chicago, IL: University of Chicago Press.

Kanter, J.W., Busch, A.M. and Rusch, L.C. (2009). *Behavioral Activation: Distinctive Features.* London and New York, NY: Routledge.

Kessler, R.C., Chiu, W.T., Demler, O., Merikangas, K.R. and Walters, E.E. (2005). Prevalence, Severity, and Comorbidity of 12-month DSM-IV Disorders in the National Comorbidity Survey Replication, *Archives of General Psychiatry*, (June) 62(6): 593–602.

LeDoux, J. (1996). *The Emotional Brain: The Mysterious Underpinnings of Emotional Life.* New York, NY: Simon & Schuster.

Malott, R.W., Whaley, D.L. and Malott, M.E. (1997). *Elementary Principles of Behavior* (third edition). Upper Saddle River, NJ: Prentice Hall.

Maslow, A. (1966). *The Psychology of Science: A Reconnaissance.* New York, NY: Harper & Row.

Mischel, W. (2014). *The Marshmallow Test: Understanding Self-control and How To Master It.* London: Bantam Press.

Mowrer, O.H. (1947). On the dual nature of learning: A reinterpretation of "conditioning" and "problem solving", *Harvard Educational Review*, 17: 102–148.

Ost, L.G. and Sterner, U. (1987). Applied tension: a specific behavioral method for treatment of blood phobia, *Behavioral Research and Therapy*, 25(1): 25–29.

Seligman, M. (2006). *Learned Optimism: How to Change Your Mind and Your Life.* New York, NY: Vintage Books.

Shapiro, F.R. (2008). Who Wrote the Serenity Prayer? The inspiring text—long attributed to an eminent theologian—may have deeper roots than we thought, *Yale Alumni Magazine*, July/August: 32–41. Available at: http://archives.yalealumnimagazine.com/issues/2008_07/serenity.html.

Shapiro, F.R. (2014). Who Wrote the Serenity Prayer? (April 28) *The Chronicle of Higher Education*. Available at: http://www.chronicle.com/article/Who-Wrote-the-Serenity-Prayer-/146159.

Taylor, G., McNeill, A., Girling, A., Farley, A., Lindson-Hawley, N. and Aveyard, P. (2014). Change in mental health after smoking cessation: systematic review and meta-analysis, *BMJ*, 348: g1151.

Twain, M. (1986 [1894]). *Pudd'nhead Wilson and Those Extraordinary Twins.* London: Penguin Classics.

Wolpe, J. (1969). *The Practice of Behavior Therapy.* New York, NY: Pergamon.

Note to Mental Health Professionals

This book focuses on key coping skills for anxiety, which are presented in an easy to remember format (i.e., the ABCS). The primary readership is the individuals who suffer with anxiety and stress disorders, along with related problems. However, the book may also prove helpful to the mental health professionals who work with these individuals. The book is useful in therapy as you can assign readings as homework for your patients, and then develop an individualized version of the ABCS for each patient to use in everyday life. You have my permission to copy and use the exercises in this book to assist you in your clinical work with patients.

The typical 300–400 page therapy books are not written in such a way that will allow a patient to easily read them and then write their own executive summary prior to memorizing the key points. This book is well-grounded in CBT research literature, but it is not an academic treatise. It has a very practical focus. One of the reasons why therapy sometimes fails is that the patient does not adequately understand what the key coping skills are and then does not get adequate practice in applying those skills. This book has a keen focus on key coping skills and presents practice exercises at the end of each chapter. As you are no doubt aware, many excellent CBT handbooks have been developed, and there are a number of handbooks each aimed at the treatment of one specific disorder: for example, the series titled Treatments That Work, edited by David H. Barlow, PhD, and also the compilation of treatment manuals by Andrews et al. (2003). Many individuals with anxiety disorders can make very large gains with these treatments (Butler et al., 2006 and Hofmann and Smits, 2008). This book takes a much broader approach, and the coping skills can be tailored to any individual with any anxiety disorder: it is based on over 40 years of experience in applying behavior therapy and CBT principles to treatment.

The material in the book has been developed over the years and has been revised and improved repeatedly, to make it more and more effective in helping people change. In recent years, leaders in the field of CBT have called for a more comprehensive, or universal, approach to the treatment of anxiety and other emotional problems. In light of this, this book has a broader focus than single-issue books that address only one anxiety disorder. Instead, the approach here is to describe a universal set of coping skills (the ABCS) for treating all primary anxiety disorders. The coping skills are then tailored to the specific disorder(s) and to the particular patient. These basic, and universal, coping skills are easy to remember and, with appropriate tailoring, work for the treatment of each anxiety disorder and for each particular patient. When patients have multiple anxiety disorders, the format of the ABCS makes it easier for the patient to understand how each disorder is best handled.

Once you have made a careful and comprehensive diagnosis (or diagnoses) of the patient's condition (or conditions) you can match it to the specific ABCS that the patient will need to learn and use. You can make the ABCS even more specific to the patient you are working with by including their own information in the appropriate place. For example the patient who is having trouble accepting some aspect of their reality can be given an ABCS handout that includes acceptance of the specific situation (e.g., a newly diagnosed disease or a spouse's desire to seek a divorce, etc.). Each of the four basic coping skills that make up the ABCS work best when they are tailored specifically to the patient, using the patient's own experiences and information to personalize them.

If a psychologist or therapist treats the patient for only one disorder and leaves other disorders untreated then that can leave the patient with unresolved issues. Comorbidity, where an individual has two or more mental health or substance abuse disorders, has been reported to occur in 45% of all individuals who have one or more disorders (Kessler et al., 2005). Experienced clinicians often estimate much higher rates of comorbidity, since many of the individuals who enter outpatient treatment cannot be neatly placed into only one diagnostic category. In my own practice, I reviewed the first ten files in my open case file drawer. Nine of those ten patients had more than one disorder. In most of those cases the same patient had two or more anxiety disorders and a diagnosis of an accompanying mood disorder. Several of the cases included problems with the expression of anger. Finally, several of the cases also had a history of a substance abuse disorder. For many years I have attempted to assess and then provide comprehensive treatment for all the disorders that a patient faces. David H. Barlow has written and spoken about the need for a "unified protocol" to address all of the primary problems that are presented in a typical case rather than just treating one disorder (Barlow et al., 2011). I believe that this type of comprehensive approach can provide better treatment and more resistance to relapse.

The availability of CBT trained professionals does not seem to be sufficient for the prevalence of anxiety disorders that we are now seeing. It seems clear that there is a need for many more well-trained cognitive behavioral therapists to be available in each community in order for individuals to receive adequate treatment. That means there needs to be more public support for graduate schools to increase the number of CBT slots that are available and to make the training of CBT psychologists, social workers and other therapists a priority. In addition, there needs to be more public education to further increase awareness of anxiety disorders and to advocate for treating individuals who suffer from anxiety disorders with the same respect given to those who suffer with physical problems. Hopefully in the future we will be in a position where everyone who requires access to CBT will be able to get it. In the meantime, this book is my small contribution to making the principles of this therapy more widely available.